The first time that I really saw Michael Jackson was backstage at The Hollywood Palace in 1969. You could see then that there were plans for Michael, that he would emerge as a major star. I think that when a person has "star quality," he will find a way to get himself out there in the forefront, and that is exactly what Michael has done. He just has so much creativity that it came out at an early age and continued to evolve. Michael's career is what every artist would love for his own career to become, a career that takes on a natural progression and allows his creativity to grow. As long as he does not become lost in the world of entertainment, if he can keep his feet on the ground, and as long as he continues to love it, he can go on and always be beautiful!

What Mark Bego has written in this book is an in-depth look at Michael Jackson, and I hope you enjoy it.

Mary Wilson
of The Supremes
Fall 1983

Michael!

by Mark Bego

PINNACLE BOOKS **NEW YORK**

MICHAEL!

An original Pinnacle Books edition, published for the first time anywhere.

First printing, March 1984

ISBN: 0-523-4223402

Can. ISBN: 0-523-43223-2

Cover photo by Ebet Roberts

Printed in the United States of America

PINNACLE BOOKS, INC.
1430 Broadway
New York, New York 10018

9 8 7 6 5 4 3 2 1

Acknowledgements:

The author would like to thank these people for their help and assistance in the completion of this book:

Bart Andrews, John Benitez, Gail Chancey, Frankie Crocker, Jack Cunningham, Ron & Betty Galella, Roger Glazer, Raymond Griffis, Elliot Hubbard, Harry Haun, LaToya Jackson, Randy Jones, Jill Klein, Suzan Kressel, June Lazarus, Barbara Ligeti, Jim Lopes, Sue McDonald, Charles Moniz, Marie Morreale, John Paxton, Marisa Redanty, Kenneth Reynolds, Sherry Robb, David Salidor, Jay Schwartz, Jarvey Schwartzberg, Barbara Shelley, Russell Turiak, Sarah Uman, Kelly West, Mary Wilson.

Material for this book has been gathered in first-hand personal interviews, and information from the following publications:

Billboard, Black Radio Exclusive, Black Stars, Cash Box The Chicago Times, Circus, Creem, The Detroit Free Press, Entertainment Rap, High Fidelity, Interview, The Los Angeles Herald Examiner, The Los Angeles Times, Life, The New York Daily News, The New York Post, The New York Times, Newsweek, People, Playgirl, Rock & Soul, Rolling Stone, Seventeen, Soul, Stars & Superstars Of Black Music, Stereo Review, Teen Bag, Time, TV Movie Picture Life, US, USA Today, Variety, The Village Voice.

*In memory of my dear friend
Barbra Nagel.*

Contents

Michael!

Introduction

Ever since he burst onto the music scene in 1969 as the eleven-year-old lead singer of *The Jackson Five*, Michael Jackson has owned the hearts of millions of fans around the world of every age, race and musical taste. Today, at the age of 25, Michael is an award-winning best-selling singer, songwriter, producer, movie star, and avowed show business master-of-all-trades!

With his 1979 eight million-selling album "Off The Wall," Michael became the first solo artist to have four "Top Ten" hits released off of one album. In 1983 he broke this record with his ten million-selling album "Thriller" and it's five "Top Ten" smashes "Billie Jean," "The Girl Is Mine," "Beat it," "Wanna Be Startin' Something," and "Human Nature."

This feat has made him the first solo artist in the history of recorded music to have five "Top Ten" singles released from one album, and "Thriller" has also become the largest selling album by a male recording artist. Michael's only solo rival in making him *The* top record-breaker is Carole King and her 1971 classic album "Tapestry," with total sales at fifteen million units sold world-wide. "Thriller" is likely to exceed that number as well. The only two albums to have sold more than that are the soundtrack albums to the movies "Saturday Night Fever" and "Grease," which have sold approximately twenty-five million copies apiece. Both of these albums were two-record sets by various artists.

Michael was one of the stars of the motion picture version of the Broadway smash "The Wiz," he hangs out with Jane Fonda and Steven Spielberg, he gossips on the phone with Liza Minnelli and Adam Ant, dates Tatum O'Neil, produces hit songs for his best friend Diana Ross, and Katharine Hepburn visits him backstage when he headlines Madison Square Garden.

Michael Jackson is recognized as the decade's biggest superstar, and his story is a phenomenal legacy of talent, work, and creative perfection!

When Diana Ross & *The Supremes* introduced them on ABC-TV's "The Hollywood Palace" in October of 1969, *Jackson Five*-mania and Michael's grooming toward superstardom began. Within the next year their hit singles "I Want You Back," "ABC," "The Love You Save," and "I'll Be There" all reached the Number One spot on both the "Pop" and "Soul" record charts, and were all certified "Platinum" for sales figures of two million plus!

In 1971 it was "Mama's Pearl," "Never Can Say

Goodbye," "Maybe Tomorrow" and "Sugar Daddy," and in 1972 it was "Little Bitty Pretty One," "Lookin' Through The Windows" and "Corner of The Sky" all reaching the nation's "Top Twenty" charts! It was in 1971 that Michael, while singing all of the lead vocals for *The Jackson Five*'s hits, began his simultaneous solo career with his smashes "Got To Be There," "I Wanna Be Where You Are," "Rockin' Robin," "One Day In Your Life," and the two million-selling Number One hit "Ben" from the movie of the same name.

Within that two-year span, Michael, along with his brothers Jermaine, Jackie, Tito and Marlon as *The Jackson Five*, appeared on every major television show, and starred in their own network special entitled "Goin' Back To Indiana." This same period also saw the debut of "The Jackson Five" Saturday morning television cartoon series.

Amid Motown Records' vast success with such stars as *The Supremes, The Temptations* and Stevie Wonder just to name a few, Michael and *The Jackson Five* claimed the distinction of being the fastest-selling act in Motown's history. After nine more chart singles for Michael, solo and with his brothers, there was parting of the ways with Motown, and *The Jackson Five* was no more. Michael's younger brother Randy had begun touring with his brothers in 1973, so when the split came, Michael, Tito, Jackie, Marlon and Randy moved to Epic Records as *The Jacksons,* and Jermaine remained at Motown as a solo artist.

The 1976 Michael and *The Jacksons* returned to the "Top Ten" with their million-selling smash Epic Records debut "Enjoy Yourself" from their album "The Jacksons." In 1977 they released their second Epic album

"Goin' Places." Both Epic albums were produced by the Philadelphia hit-making team Gamble & Huff, but Michael and his brothers longed to branch out into their own writing and producing. This dream came true in 1978 with the release of their most successful group album to date, "Destiny." The song that Michael and Randy wrote, "Shake Your Body (Down to The Ground)" sold two million copies and gave Michael the bug for further composing.

1978 saw the release of "The Wiz," the film that marked Michael's movie debut, co-starring such talents as Diana Ross, Richard Pryor and Lena Horne. The project also teamed him with producer Quincy Jones for the first time.

Michael's subsequent work with Quincy in 1979's "Off The Wall" and 1982's "Thriller" have made Michael the best-selling recording artist on the scene today!

In July of 1983 *Cash Box* magazine, in their Annual Awards Special Edition, distinguished Michael Jackson with the following honors:

—#1 Male Artist
—#1 Pop Single ("Billie Jean")
—#1 Male Singles Artist
—#1 Black Album ("Thriller")
—#1 Pop Album ("Thriller")
—#1 Black Male Artist
—#1 Black Male Singles Artist
—#1 Black Single ("Billie Jean")

With the recent confirmation that Michael Jackson will continue his film career by starring in and handling the soundtrack of Steven Spielberg's new production of the classic ''Peter Pan,'' its clear that his multi-media pursuits have just begun!

Ladies and gentlemen: Presenting ''Michael!''—The Michael Jackson Story . . .

1

Meet Michael Jackson

"All children, except one, grow up."

This is the opening sentence of J.M. Barrie's immortally imaginative classic, "Peter Pan." It is Michael Jackson's favorite book.

Michael, at the age of twenty-five, and the pinnacle of his multi-media career is readying himself to film his first title role starring motion picture. Although he has taken the country by storm with his electrifyingly charismatic and self-confident performances on the video presentations of "Beat It" and "Billie Jean," and on his performance on the Motown 25th Anniversary television special, he is in fact a very shy and lonely young man.

He lives in Encino, California with his two younger sisters, minutes away from Hollywood. "I think I'd die on my own. I'd be so lonely. Even at home, I'm lonely. I sit in my room sometimes and cry. It's so hard to make friends, and there are some things you can't talk to your parents or family about. I sometimes walk around the neighborhood at night, just hoping to find someone to talk to. But I just end up coming home.''

One minute he's the sexy spinning singer emotionally lacerating his fans with sass and assuredness, the next he is lonely and dejected and doesn't know what direction to turn. It is logical to ask if there is a clear-cut answer to the question; Where does Michael Jackson end and Peter Pan begin? Their similarities are uncanny!

In 1978, in his film debut as The Scarecrow in Sidney Lumet's production of ''The Wiz,'' Michael was cast so perfectly as a sheltered inhabitant of the Emerald City of Oz that at the end of each day's shooting, he had to be coerced into removing his make-up and costume, and into leaving the fantasy-like set.

''What's wonderful about a film,'' Michael analyzes, ''is that you can become another person. I love to forget. And lots of times, you *totally* forget.''

He continues, ''I love putting on an outfit or a costume and just looking at myself in the mirror. Baggy pants or some real funky shoes and a hat and just feeling the character of it. That's fun to me. I love it so much. It's escape. It's fun. It's just neat to become another thing, another person. Especially when you really believe it and it's not like you're acting. I always hated the word 'acting'—to say, 'I'm an actor.' It should be more than that. It should be more like a believer.''

In 1982, when Michael went into the recording studio to narrate and sing on the Quincy Jones/Steven Spielberg storybook record project, ''E.T.: The Extra Terrestrial,'' he also had trouble differentiating fiction from fact, or rather preferred to believe the imaginary.

If he had his choice, he would have remained in that storybook forest with his new-found friend.

"That's what I loved about doing 'E.T.!' " says Michael, "I was actually there. The next day, I missed him a lot. I wanted to go back to that spot I was at yesterday in the forest. I wanted to be there."

When he encountered the plastic E.T. model for the publicity photo session, he explains, "He grabbed me, he put his arms around me. He was so real that I was talking to him. I kissed him before I left."

"The first time I saw 'E.T.,' " says Michael of the movie. "I melted through the whole thing. The second time, I cried like crazy. And then, in doing the narration, I felt like I was there with them, like behind the tree or something, watching everything that happened."

Before the project was over, Steven Spielberg told Michael, "If E.T. didn't come to Elliott, he would have come to your house!"

Spielberg feels that, "Michael is one of the last living innocents who is in complete control of his life. I've never seen *anybody* like Michael. He's an emotional star child."

"He's in full control," Steven continues, "Sometimes he appears to other people to be sort of wavering on the fringes of twilight, but there is great conscious forethought behind everything he does. He's very smart about his career and the choices he makes. I think he is definitely a man of two personalities."

"I hate to admit it," says Michael of the paradox, "but I feel strange around everyday people. See, my whole life has been onstage. And the impression I get of people is applause, standing ovations and running after you. In a crowd I'm afraid. Onstage I feel safe. If I could I would sleep on the stage. I'm serious."

For this reason, whenever he can be, Michael regenerates his energy by being alone in his fantasy world.

He is having his home re-done . . . by Disneyland! "Disney Studios is building a whole 'Pirates Of The Caribbean' in the entry hall of the house." he explains, "There will be robots that talk and sing and shoot guns and dance. You'll walk into the middle of this whole fantasy war and smoke and cannons and everything!"

Continuing to explain his sheltered lifestyle, he adds, "I love to read. I like philosophy and short stories. I like to keep up with the latest best-sellers. *The Calendar* in the Sunday *L.A. Times* is my favorite paper. It really lets you know what's going on everywhere. I have my favorite authors—it's not like I just read the best-sellers. I like to see what they are doing and keep up with what people are interested in."

"Every Sunday I dance for thirty minutes straight without stopping . . . sometimes to my own music, sometimes to any fast beat. That's just the day I pick. Like I fast every Sunday. I don't eat anything. Just juices. I think it's a great feeling. People should clean the toxins out of their systems. It helps keep you strong."

There are drawbacks to fame, especially if you want to go in public and not be recognized. Says Michael, "It never has bothered me except sometimes when you want peace. Like you go to the theater and you say, 'Nobody's bothering me tonight, I'm wearing a hat and glasses and I'm going to enjoy this film and that's all there is to it.' You get in there and everybody's watching and staring at you and at the climax of the film somebody taps you on the shoulder for an autograph. You just feel like you can't get away."

According to Diana Ross, "He spends a lot of time, too much time, by himself. I try to get him out. I rented a boat and took my children and Michael on a cruise. Michael has a lot of people around him, but he's very afraid. I don't know why. I think it came from the early days."

Of his own self-protective hibernation, Michael admits to keeping to himself, "just like a hemophiliac who can't afford to be scratched in any way."

When he's off in his own little world, Michael has three indulgences of fantasy that he allows into his realm. The first two are animals and (like Peter Pan) children.

His own personal menagerie includes a boa constrictor named Muscles whom Michael will introduce by explaining compassionately that, "Snakes are very misunderstood," a sheep named Mr. Tibbs, and a llama named Louie.

"I think they're sweet," says Michael of his animal friends, "I like to pry into their world and watch the way they move about. I just stare at them."

Of his fascination with children, he explains, "When I'm upset about a recording session, I'll dash off on my bike and ride to the schoolyard, just to be around them. When I come back to the studio, I'm ready to move mountains. Kids do that to me. It's like magic."

"Know what I also love?" asks Michael, exposing his third fantasy realm, "Mannequins. I guess I want to bring them to life." He shares his living quarters with several life-size mannequins and explains why he likes them. "I like to imagine talking to them. You know what I think it is? Yeah, I think I'll say it. I think I'm accompanying myself with friends I never had. I probably have two friends. And I just got them. Being an entertainer, you just can't tell who is your friend. And they see you so differently. A star instead of a next-door neighbor. That's what it is. I surround myself with people I want to be my friends. And I can do that with mannequins, I'll talk to them.''

''I'm a collector of cartoons,'' says Michael of another fantasy preoccupation. ''All the Disney stuff, Bugs Bunny, the old MGM ones. I've only met one person who has a bigger collection than I do, and I was surprised. Paul McCartney, he's a cartoon fanatic! Whenever I go to his house, we watch cartoons. When we came here to work on my album, we rented all these cartoons from the studio; Dumbo and some other stuff. It's real escapism. It's like everything's all right. It's like the world is happening now in a faraway city. Everything's fine.''

''Magic is easy if you put your heart into it,'' he claims, only affirming that he is the perfect person to become the embodiment of Peter Pan's latest incarnation.

''We *can* fly, you know,'' he continues. ''We just don't know how to think the right thoughts and levitate ourselves off the ground.''

''I love Steven,'' says Michael of director Spielberg. ''I will say Steven is my favorite director, and that he's looked long and hard for the right property. I've always wanted to go into film, musicals, and do the scoring, to act in it, to choreograph it. That's my all-time love. Jane Fonda is a good friend of mine and we talk about acting. She's one of the greats of our age. She and Vivien Leigh and Bette Davis and Katharine Hepburn and Cicely Tyson. There have been so many great offers since I did "The Wiz." I've been asked to do "A Chorus Line," the Broadway show; and "Mr. Bojangles," the life of Bill Robinson.

"My room is loaded with scripts and offers. And a lot of them are great ideas. But the kind of person I am is that I have a person in mind that I'd like to work with and I'm trying to make sure I do the right thing. I just don't want to make a mistake."

The film version of the award-winning Broadway show about Broadway 'gypsies,' "A Chorus Line" has been discussed in Hollywood circles since the show opened in New York City in 1975, and now it is the longest-running musical in Broadway history! In 1978, after "The Wiz" was released, Sidney Lumet reportedly offered Michael the role of Paul in the movie version of "A Chorus Line," which Sammy Williams originated on Broadway. In the plot of the show each of the characters are seeking dancing roles in one particular show. Through the basis of their intense audition, each of them exposes their own hopes, fears and insecurities. In the show Paul confesses as part of his self-examining catharsis, that he is gay.

At the time Michael told Hollywood syndicated columnist Marilyn Beck that "I'm excited about it, but if I do it, people will link me with the part. Because of my voice, some people already think I'm that way—homo. Though, I'm actually not at all. It's just a lot of gossip, which isn't important. The only thing that is important is that I do what I want—act, sing and dance."

It was Jane Fonda who originally connected Michael

with "Peter Pan." When Michael visited Jane on the set of "On Golden Pond," Michael became very friendly with Henry Fonda. Jane observed, "Dad was also painfully self-conscious and shy in life, and he really only felt comfortable when he was behind the mask of a character. He could liberate himself only when he was being someone else. That's a lot like Michael."

"In some ways Michael reminds me of the walking wounded," Jane continued, "He's an extremely fragile person. I think that just getting on with life, making contact with people, is hard enough, much less to be worried about whither goest the world.

"I remember driving with him one day, and I said, 'God, Michael, I wish I could find a movie I could produce for you.' And suddenly I knew. I said, 'I know what you've got to do. It's 'Peter Pan.' Tears welled up in his eyes and he said, 'Why did you say that?' with this ferocity. I said, 'I realize *you're* Peter Pan.' And he started to cry and said, 'You know, all over the walls of my room are pictures of Peter Pan. I've read everything that Barrie wrote. I totally identify with Peter Pan, the lost boy of Never-Neverland.' Oh, I can see him leading-lost children into a world of fantasy and magic. From Gary, straight on to Barrie!" Jane exclaims.

In June of 1983 it was confirmed that Michael would be starring in "Peter Pan," but it was unclear who would be credited as producer. Steven Spielberg, Francis Ford Coppola, Jane Fonda, or all three may have decided to do it . . . but it is in the works.

How does Michael feel about his scizophrenic image? "I don't mind." he says, "I feel I'm Peter Pan as well as Methusaleh, and a child!" Look out Captain Hook . . . here comes Michael Jackson!

However, it wasn't all that long ago that the glamorous world of show business was as distant as Never-Neverland to a little boy in Gary, Indiana. Let's go all the way back to the very beginnings of *The Jackson Five* in a working class city near Lake Michigan, and trace the path that led young Michael Joseph Jackson to the heights of international superstardom . . .

2

The Jackson Five's Early Years

Gary, Indiana is a very gray, industrial town, south of Chicago, Illinois. It was there that Joe Jackson, and his wife Katherine lived with their nine children.

In the 1950's Joe had aspirations of going into show business, but the realities of his growing family forced him to put these dreams aside. He had sung and played guitar in a blues group that called themselves *The Falcons* which, as he recalls, "mostly worked colleges and bars." Soon, the responsibility of eleven mouths to feed, made "music" something that came out of the radio, instead of a career. Joe supported his family as a crane operator, and his once-precious guitar was relegated to a life of collecting dust in a closet.

Katherine remembers singing around the house, and teaching her children songs to sing along with her. "It was just plain stuff," she recalls, but it was in this atmosphere that young Michael Jackson was exposed to and became interested in music.

As Michael tells it; "My father had a group called *The Falcons*; they were three brothers and they played guitars and sang, so there was always a guitar lying around. We started out singing at home. I was five-years-old in the beginning. My brother Tito would pick up the guitar and play, and eventually we would start singing to the playing. We would sing songs like 'Cotton Fields Back Home' and some old Ray Charles and James Brown stuff. One day my father caught Tito with the guitar and he got so mad because he didn't want anybody to touch his beautiful guitar. It was something that he cherished, and he kept it as a memory piece.

"When he found Tito playing it he let him have it! Then he said to Tito, 'Let me see what you can do!' and he meant it. Well, Tito whipped out the guitar and started really playing. My father was shocked, because he saw some special talent there. He was really surprised, and he was so happy that his son could do this!"

Soon a group was formed in the household, with Jackie, Jermaine and Tito. Next, Marlon joined in, and young Michael would pound on a set of bongos while his older brothers performed.

One day his mother was startled to hear young Michael imitating Jermaine's singing, and told her husband, "I think we have another lead singer!"

Jackie recalls; "He was so energetic that at five-years-old he was like a leader, we saw that. So, we said, 'Hey, Michael, you be the lead guy.'" And so, history was made!

Soon Joe was encouraging his boys to pursue music, and he began to spend his hard earned money for instruments. Katherine did protest at first, but eventually gave in to her husband's preoccupation with their children's new-found hobby. "When a woman's a good mother and finds all the money going for instruments, she doesn't like it," Joe admitted, but he encouraged them further.

Says Tito of the experience, "Our parents did push us, but it wasn't against our will. We loved music. It was a thrill to be making music at that age that sounded good and that the adults seemed to like. The other kids would pass by our house on the way home from school and they'd see us practicing every day. Some of them stopped to listen. Others would make fun. They'd say, 'Look at those Jacksons. They won't get anywhere. They're just doing all that for nothing.' But we kept at it. I think a lot of our success now is because we got started so early."

Soon the whole family became enthused by the music. Says Joe; "If you're around something a lot, you're gonna take part in it." Besides, it was a perfect outlet to keep the boys occupied with something constructive after school. "In Gary," explains Joe, "with all the steel mills, kids don't have anything to do except go to school and come home. So they learn how to sing or play some type of instrument. The kids want to better their condition, because they see their parents working every day in the mills."

Michael doesn't remember much before that, "Actually I was so small I don't remember. When I was five I was touring, singing and dancing. Always gone, always out of school. I just remember little things like the corner store or certain people in the neighborhood.The high school behind us always had a big band with trumpets and trombones and drums coming down the street. I used to love that, like a parade. I still remember the first time I sang in kindergarten class. I sang 'Climb Every Mountain,' and everyone got excited!

"A lady in the neighborhood came up with the name *The Jackson Five*. We started rehearsing every day after school. Kids would tease us because we would be rehearsing all the time, even in school. There was a big baseball park behind our house and we would hear the roar of the crowd, and we would be inside rehearsing and this would get us mad. Rocks would come through the window, people would tease us, but eventually it all paid off. We got a lot in exchange for not playing baseball in the summer!"

According to Jackie, "We always knew we were going to hit it big. It was just a matter of getting the breaks."

Their lucky breaks came at first in the form of local talent shows.

Michael remembers, "Every time there was a talent show, everyone on our block would go and try for a trophy. We learned at an early age that people don't just give you a chance; you have to win it. Everybody around us was trying to get into some type of show business. My father was always very protective of us, taking care of business and everything. We went to school, but I guess we were even different then, because everyone in the neighborhood knew about us. We'd win every talent show and our house was loaded with trophies."

Says Jackie, "In our block there were a lot of groups competing. Every time there was a talent show, everyone would come to try for the trophy. Deniece Williams was one of them, and Kellee Patterson.''

"When we sang,'' says Michael, "people would throw all this money on the floor, tons of dollars, tens, twenties, lots of change. I remember my pockets being so full of money that I couldn't keep my pants up. I'd wear a real tight belt, and I'd buy candy like crazy!''

He also remembers sharing it with others. "We always had money and we could always buy things the other kids couldn't, like extra candy and extra bubblegum. Our pockets were always loaded and we'd be passing out candy. That made us popular!'' he exclaims.

The Jackson Five soon found itself on a winning streak. "I think the first paying gig we had was at a place called Mr. Lucky's. We started to see that we had real possibilities,'' Michael explains.

Katherine Jackson, however remembers her concern for her five-year-old son, Michael. "It was sort of frightening,'' she says. "He was so young. He didn't go out and play much. So if you want me to tell you the truth, I don't know where he got it. He just knew.''

Yes, even then Michael knew that what he was doing was special.

Katherine continues, "Every time I'd go to a concert I'd worry, because sometimes the girls would get on-stage and I'd have to watch them tearing at Michael. He was so small, and they were so big.''

Michael began to pick-up things from other performers that he would see from the wings of the theaters *The Jackson Five* were performing in. "Soon we were doing theaters,'' he recalls, "and 'Amateur Hour' with James Brown . . . Jackie Wilson . . . Gladys Knight.''

Looking back, Gladys recalls, "We go back a really

long way. I'm talking about our theater days, you know, when the Jacksons used to come up to the Regal Theater in Chicago. I remember Michael's legs weren't long enough to reach the floor when he was sitting down!''

The more he performed, the more Michael liked it. "My dad taught me how to work the mike and things like that," he says. "And, I learned a lot about dancing and moving around from watching James Brown and Sammy Davis on television.''

Michael admits to this day; "I always enjoyed the feeling of being on stage—the magic that comes. When I hit the stage it's like all of a sudden a magic from somewhere just comes and the spirit hits you and you just lose control of yourself.

"Something is really missing when I'm not on stage. It may sound crazy, but I'm a stage addict. When I'm not on stage for a long time I have fits and I get crazy. I start crying and I act . . . I guess you might say 'weird' and 'freaked out.' I start dancing around the house. It's like a part of me is missing and I have this wild craving for it.

"On stage is the only time I really open up. I say to myself, 'This is it. This is home. This is where I'm supposed to be, where God meant me to be.' I feel so free, so unlimited on stage. I feel like I can do anything. It feels so good when the lights hit you and you feel the audience. I eat it up. Performing is better than anything else I can think of!'' Michael insists.

It's easy to see that an audience has always been able to pick-up on Michael's kinetic energy on stage. When he's having fun in front of the spotlights, the crowd does too, and they always have. However, commercial success wasn't an overnight transition. *The Jackson Five* performed together for five years, gradually gaining experience and recognition. They worked every gig they could. They were booked in places all over Illinois, Indiana and Wisconsin, plus a couple of faraway places like New York and Arizona. Once they were an opening act at New York City's famed Apollo Theater in Harlem. Michael says he will always remember watching James Brown perform. "He's so magic. I'd be in the wings when I was like six or seven. I'd sit there and watch him!"

Popular New York radio personality, Frankie Crocker of Manhattan's WBLS-FM, remembers that the first time he met Michael was backstage at that very same engagement. According to Frankie, Michael had all of the earmarkings of stardom just in the way he sang and the way he moved. Says Crocker, "I've known Michael, since he was nine, and we both were working at the Apollo Theater . . . I think it was 1967 or 1968. At that time, he was just a kid, and he was playful. He used to play 'tag' a lot: he'd hit you and run upstairs. He was very small. He was slight at the time; a real little kid. You could see then that he had a lot of the moves. *The Jackson Five* had a big impact on music. They were a good-looking family of young men . . . very professional on stage, great visually, and the music struck a chord in American youth that catapulted them to superstardom."

"Everyone thinks we started at the top," says Marlon, setting the record straight, "but we traveled around for years before that—five brothers and two sisters—crammed into a Volkswagen van. We played around our home town of Gary, but we also went out to Kansas City and

St. Louis. We'd get home at five in the morning a lot of times, then get up the next day and go to school. We're used to hard work.''

The first time that record producer Freddie Perren saw *The Jackson Five*, he was in Jerry Butler's band. Ironically he was one of the writers that came to call themselves "The Corporation," and wrote many of *The Jackson Five*'s biggest hits. Freddie remembers them as the opening act, "I was a pianist with Jerry Butler in 1968 and we were playing a club in Chicago . . . That was Jerry's hometown, so he was very popular. When I saw these little kids opening the show for us, I really felt sorry for them and hoped the crowd would be kind to them. Michael was so little and innocent. Well, they just destroyed the audience. He was just an amazing performer. Hey, it was very tough trying to come on after that, let me tell you.''

In Gary, *The Jackson Five* grabbed every chance they could get to perform, including benefits for Muigwighania, a local Black pride organization which was headed by an aspiring politician named Richard Hatcher. In 1968, Hatcher was campaigning to become Gary, Indiana's first Black mayor, and invited *The Jackson Five* to entertain at one of his campaign rally's. Also on the bill was *Diana Ross & The Supremes*: Mary Wilson and Cindy Birdsong. When Diana saw Michael and his brothers perform she flipped, and immediately got Berry Gordy, Jr., the president of Motown Records on the phone to tell him what she had seen. She made arrangements for *The Jackson Five* to audition for Motown at Berry's home in Detroit.

Diana remembers, ''I looked at this little kid whirling around up there and I thought I was looking at myself. I couldn't believe it. I thought the group was terrific, so I asked them if they'd like to meet the head of my record company, Berry Gordy, Jr. I saw so much of myself as a child in Michael. He was performing all the time. That's the way I was. He could be my son." And so was born a lifelong bond between Diana and Michael.

Joseph Jackson remembers it like this: "Let me put it this way, we were at the gate. To me it seemed there was an iron gate in the entertainment field. And there just had to be a way to open that gate before you could get through. We sorta had one foot in and then along came Diana Ross. What she did for my boys was to open that gate. Yes, I have to say, Diana opened the gate for *The Jackson Five*."

Recalls Jackie of their audition, "I remember the first time we went to Berry Gordy's house in Detroit. It was the biggest place we had ever seen. His backyard was like a golf course and he had an indoor pool. He had us entertain at a party and most of the Motown artists were there. That's what really scared us. We were up there doing their songs!"

According to Michael, "We auditioned for Motown at Berry Gordy's mansion in Detroit among all the Motown stars: *The Temptations*, Diana Ross, *The Marvelettes*, people that we admired. We did our show and they loved it. They gave us a standing ovation. Berry Gordy came over, and Diana Ross came over at the end of the show and she kissed each one of us. She said she loved what she saw and she wanted to be a part of what we do."

The Jackson family knew that they had performed very impressively, but there was a slight waiting period before they found out if they were going to get a recording contract or not. Jackie distinctively recalls "not being able to use the phone for two months while we waited to hear from Motown. We wanted to keep the line clear!"

When the call did come, the news was good, and Motown signed them to a recording contract. Although Diana Ross is often attributed with "discovering" *The Jackson Five*, Michael always clarifies the fact by saying, "Nobody discovered the Jacksons except their mother and father. We were an established professional act long before we ever signed with Motown."

"So," says Michael, "we moved to California and half of the group stayed with Diana and the other half lived with Berry Gordy. I lived with Diana for almost a year-and-a-half. It was like paradise. We went to Disneyland, we had fun every day. This was a whole other thing from Gary, Indiana. And we went into the studio and came up with 'I Want You Back.' "

Their first record wasn't an overnight success either. By 1969 Freddie Perren had signed on with Motown as a songwriter, and together with Fonce Mizell, Deke Richards and Berry Gordy himself, they became known as "The Corporation."

"Deke, Fonce and I were having a hard time getting records released," says Perren. "We were on staff at Motown in Los Angeles, but between Norman Whitfield, Smokey Robinson, etc., it was hard to get time with any of the top acts. At the time, Gladys Knight hadn't had a hit in a while, so we decided to cut a track for her." The song was called "Want To Be Free."

Freddie continues, "Berry said it was a very energetic, youthful rhythm track and he had these kids from Gary he'd like to use it on. We rewrote the song, aimed it more toward a little kid and called it 'I Want You Back.' Well, we cut it with the kids and the vocals were great. We took it back to Berry with our chests stuck out. We knew we had it. He listened to it, turned to us and said, 'You guys are ready to blow a hit.' He went over the entire record, telling us where we had messed up.''

"I Want You Back" was reworked, re-recorded, and released as the first *Jackson Five* single in the fall of 1969. The group was signed to make their American television debut in mid-autumn, 1969 on the ABC-TV series "The Hollywood Palace" with *Diana Ross & The Supremes* as the special guest hostesses.

Backstage that night at "The Hollywood Palace" *The Jackson Five* stood poised to go on stage, like a rocket ready to "blast off!" And, that's just what they were about to do. That Saturday night, October 18, 1969, the Jackon family was about to launch one of the most famous debut singles in recorded history, their two-million selling smash "I Want You Back." At the time Jackie was eighteen, Tito was sixteen, Jermaine was fifteen, Marlon was twelve, and Michael; the soon-to-be-superstar was already a seasoned performer at the age of eleven. That was the night that Michael and his brothers became bonafide stars, and their life hasn't been the same since!

3

The Jackson Five Hit The Top

That night in October of 1969, when *The Jackson Five* made their television debut on "The Hollywood Palace" it was literally "Motown At The Hollywood Palace!" In fact, a Motown album of the same name marked the event for posterity, and was released in 1970.

The show opened with *Diana Ross & The Supremes;* Mary Wilson and Cindy Birdsong, singing a medley of songs from the Broadway show "Hair." Diana sang "Where Do I Go," while Mary & Cindy joined in with "Good Morning Starshine," for the opening number.

After their "Hair" medley, Diana took the microphone and announced, "Good evening ladies and gentlemen, and welcome to 'The Hollywood Palace.' It's wonderful to return as your hostess, especially tonight, when I have the pleasure of introducing a great young star, who has been in the business all of his life. He has worked with his family, and when he sings and dances, he lights up the stage. Here he is, Michael Jackson and *The Jackson Five*.''

They proceeded to sing the ballad "Can You Remember" from their forthcoming debut album. After a warm round of applause, Michael looked right into the television camera and announced, "Now we'd like to do our very first release on Motown. It's on sale everywhere!" The quintet then dove into "I Want You Back" and tore up the stage.

Following their song and a thunderous round of applause, Diana came back on stage and spoke with Michael for a moment. She then announced, "Ladies and gentlemen, Miss Mary Wilson . . ." At that point Mary came out and sang her solo "Can't Take My Eyes Off of You." Also on the show that evening were *Gladys Knight & The Pips*, and Stevie Wonder. The show closed with Diana and *The Supremes* singing "Someday We'll Be Together." Two weeks later it was announced that Diana would be leaving *The Supremes* for a solo career.

It was a significant evening for Motown for many reasons, and Mary Wilson recalls, "I remember seeing Michael and his brothers that night at 'The Hollywood Palace.' Basically they were pretty shy little kids, and all of the attention was going toward Michael. You could see then that there were plans for Michael, that he would emerge as a major star. It was very clear to me that he would, that he actually had the capability of going on to do the type of things that Diana did. That was very noticeable. The other young fellows were like *The Supremes*—they were there, but a part of the group that was clearly centered around Michael."

"They were all shy," continues Mary, "but he was just something different. He had a 'star quality' at that age. They (his brothers) all have very distinct personalities, but they were pretty much like me; they liked being part of the group. Even though they might be very creative, they don't step forward to show their creativeness as much, and a person like a Michael, or a Diana, or like I am becoming—when you really have to be out front, you stand out even when you are not out front. They're very nice guys, all of them. You can tell they come from a good homelife, and a good family background.''

Diana's statement at the time was as follows:

"Honesty has always been a very special word for me—a very special idea. I don't necessarily mean the kind of honesty that our history books tell us Abraham Lincoln practiced—although that's fine.

"But when I think of my own personal idea of honesty, I think of something being straight out, all there, on the table—the way it is. Steak should be steak, you know what I mean? Why disguise it? If it's good steak, well, just let it be good steak.

"That's how I feel about *The Jackson Five*—five brothers by the name of Jackson who I discovered in Gary, Indiana. *The Jackson Five* sing honest. Straight out. No tricks. No gimmicks. But good. Very, very, very good.

"Everything about these guys says 'honesty' to me. Whether they're singing Smokey Robinson or *The Beatles* or an old standard, they exhibit an inborn professionalism and an inate honesty which says everything. Their young enthusiasm—and they are young—from lead singer Michael, who is ten, up through Jackie, sixteen; and including Marlon, twelve; Jermaine, thirteen; and Toriano

31

(Tito), fourteen—their clean approach, their optimistic zest . . . everything is right up front. You can't miss it. Mayor Richard Hatcher of Gary, Indiana didn't miss it. He's the one who brought *The Jackson Five* to my attention. Record producer Bobby Taylor didn't miss it. He was the first professional to work with the guys. Motown Records didn't miss it. They produced The Jackson Five's first hit single, 'I Want You Back.' No one's going to miss it. Everything about *The Jackson Five* is for real. They've got great talent. And above all they're honest.''

The first *Jackson Five* album, "Diana Ross Presents The Jackson 5" was released on December 18, 1969, and almost immediately sold two million copies! It should be noted that the group's title spelling varied from time to time. Originally it was presented as *The Jackson 5*, yet was usually spelled out as *The Jackson Five*. At one point all of their records spelled it with the numeral "5" in place of the "F" to become *The Jackson 5ive*. Any way you spell it, however, *The Jackson Five* became the fastest selling group in the history of Motown Records.

Oddly, there was only one single released from "Diana Ross Presents The Jackson 5," "I Want You Back," which hit Number One on the *Billboard* magazine singles chart the week of November 15, 1969. The album opens with a great version of one of the silliest songs in pop history, "Zip A Dee Doo Dah." However, silly as it is, it was also a single off of the first Dionne Warwick album ("Presenting Dionne Warwick"), and it certainly didn't harm her success any!

Also on the album was another tune composed by The Corporation specifically for *The Jackson Five* called

"Nobody," and several "cover" versions of other Motown artists hits. It seemed like everyone at Motown in those days was required to re-record Motown-owned songs so that the company would reap enormous amounts of money from the copyrights. On this first *Jackson Five* album are new versions of *The Four Tops'* hit "Standing In The Shadows Of Love," Stevie Wonder's "My Cherie Amour," *Rare Earth*'s "Chained," *The Temptations'* "(I Know) I'm Losing You," and a Smokey Robinson composition that *The Miracles* had recorded in 1960 called "Who's Lovin' You." The album also contains the *Sly & The Family Stone* smash "Stand."

To look back at this album from the 1980's, when everyone is artistically paralleling Diana Ross and Michael Jackson, the inclusion of "Who's Lovin' You" is ironic, because she recorded it with Mary Wilson and Florence Ballard on the album "Meet The Supremes" in 1962!

Since "Who's Lovin' You" is a straight-forward blues number, it is easy to say that the debut *Jackson Five* album is literally comprised of "something old, something new, something borrowed, and something blue!" Because that is seen as a superstition to assure good luck in a marriage, it seems that it was planned by someone to make sure that the relationship between Motown and *The Jackson Five* worked out!

Over the next year three more Motown albums were released by *The Jackson Five*. No sooner than "I Want You Back" began to descend, the title song to their second album was released: "ABC." Again the song shot up to the top of the charts, and hit the Number One spot the week of March 14, 1970.

The album "ABC" was released May 8, and was

certified "Gold" for sales in excess of 500,000 copies sold in the United States. The album included the hit "The Love You Save" backed with "I Found That Girl" that Jermaine sings lead on, and again hit Number One, on the charts.

Featured on the LP are cover versions of another *Supremes'* song, "The Young Folks," plus Stevie Wonder's "Never Had A Dream Come True," and *The Delphonics* tune, "La La Means I Love You." Like the album before it, "ABC" was produced by Hal Davis and The Corporation.

During the summer of 1970, the first single off *The Jackson Five*'s "Third Album" was released, the Number One hit "I'll Be There." Again, it was a million selling smash, and was followed by another "Mama's Pearl." Also on the "Third Album" were Jackson Five versions of the gospel tune "Oh How Happy," Simon & Garfunkel's "Bridge Over Troubled Water," and *Smokey Robinson & The Miracles'* hit "The Love I Saw In You Was Just A Mirage." In an attempt to give *The Jackson Five* some material that could be very autobiographical, The Corporation wrote them a rousing song called "Goin' Back To Indiana."

Later that year came the fourth album, "The Jackson 5 Christmas Album." The group finished 1970 with four Number One hit singles, four albums, and a following of devoted fans that stretched out around the world. Not a bad debut for Michael Jackson and his brothers the first year!

According to a statement that Berry Gordy made in 1970 with regard to the group's sound and appeal, "We're labeling it 'soul-bubblegum.' It's a style that appeals to the younger teens. We provide total guidance.

We provide their material, set their basic sound and work out the choreographic routines."

"Jackson Five-mania" was on, and 1971 was going to be even bigger! That year was highlighted by three more albums, three more Number One singles, their own network television special, a concert tour, their own animated cartoon series, and a cover story in "Life" magazine. To top it all off, "ABC" received a Grammy Award as the "Best Pop Song Of The Year" that winter.

"Never Can Say Goodbye" was released in the beginning of 1971, and by April 10 was Number One. The song was written by Clifton Davis, who later gained fame as the star of the TV series "That's My Mama" in the mid-1970's. It was the first single off of the "Maybe Tomorrow" album. The title song, "Maybe Tomorrow," peaked in July at Number Twenty on the pop charts, and Number Three on the "R&B" charts.

That spring, *The Jackson Five* appeared on Diana Ross' first solo television special, "Diana." Michael appeared in a couple of skits with Diana, and in another one with his brothers and Bill Cosby. On the show they performed two medleys: "Mama's Pearl"/"Walk On By"/"The Love You Save" and later in the show "I'll Be There"/"Feelin' Alright." Also on the show was Danny Thomas. There is a Motown soundtrack album of the show, and it provides a rare performance recording of *The Jackson Five*. The skit that Michael performed in the show later served as training for his acting career.

Spring also marked the arrival of the album "Maybe

Tomorrow,'' again produced by Hal Davis and The Corporation. Aside from the title hit and "Never Can Say Goodbye," it also contained a version of the 1950's hit "16 Candles" and *Martha & The Vandella's* hit "Honey Chile." Although they spent their first two years doing so many "cover" versions of other people's hits, *The Jackson Five* was such a fresh novelty, that they seemed to successfully make these songs uniquely their own.

The original "pressing" of the "Maybe Tomorrow" album features an 'open up' cover with a color centerfold of *The Jackson Five*. On the inside sleeve was an order form for all of the "fab" Jackson Five merchandise any fan could possibly want. It included Jackson Five notepads, stationery, concert posters, portrait photos, and individual posters of each of the brothers. Also available were copies of their own magazine entitled "TCB! Takin' Care Of Business" (another Michael Jackson/Diana Ross parallel: that was the title of a Supremes song and television special). There was also an individual fan kit on each member of the group called "Personal Soul-Mate Kits." Michael's read:

Now You Can Be MICHAEL'S PERSONAL SOUL-MATE! Yes, here's the way you can become Michael's very own Personal Soul-Mate! LOOK AT ALL YOU GET!
   —*Your own Michael Jackson Personal Soul-Mate Poem Poster! Written by Mike!*
   —*Your Michael Jackson Personal Soul-Mate wallet size ID card. It has a photo of Michael and his autograph!*
   —*A giant (12 × 18!) Personal Soul-Mate Poster of Michael!*

—*A portrait-size (5 × 7!) signed photo of Michael!*
—*9 different wallet-size photos of Michael!*
—*65 (just count them!) Official Michael Jackson Soul-Mate letter seal stickers! All 65 have Michael's photo! Great for all your letters to Michael and* The Jackson Five!

Plus! A Personal Letter From Michael Himself! 79 Things In All! For Only $2.00! Don't Wait!
YOU'LL LOVE BEING MICHAEL'S PERSONAL
SOUL-MATE! SEND AWAY NOW!

And you thought that Michael Jackson-mania started with "Billie Jean." No way . . . he was a teen idol before he was a teen!

However the best sales pitch comes under "The Jackson Five Official Concert Poster." It says:

—*Shows* The Jackson Five *doing their beautiful onstage thing! On Poster Paper!*
—*Put it on your Wall! Dig It Every Day!*
—*Your friends will blow their minds when they see it!*

In the early 1970's Michael and *The Jackson Five* were blowing more than minds, they were blowing the competition off of the charts!

In September of 1971, *The Jackson Five*'s fifth album hit the record stores. It was entitled "Goin' Back To Indiana" and was the soundtrack to their TV special of the same name. Also on the show was Bill Cosby, Tom Smothers, Bobby Darin, and a brief appearance by Diana Ross. Aside from the musical segments, there was also a comedy skit entitled "The Day Basketball Was Saved." It featured the basketball "Dream Team" of professionals: Rosey Grier, Bill Russell, Elvin Hayes, Elgin Baylor, and Ben Davidson.

In the basketball skit, The Dream Team were about to challenge *The Jackson Five* in a game, but feared that they would get beaten. They made a deal with the local candy and popcorn vendor to let the Jackson's eat all of the junkfood they wanted, so they would be so full that they couldn't play ball. However the plan backfired because Jackie was absent from the eat-a-thon, and he was the star dribbler of the family.

Aside from their own hits, on the show they also performed two *Sly & The Family Stone* songs, "Stand" and "I Want To Take You Higher, and Dave Mason's "Feelin' Alright."

That same month, *The Jackson Five* appeared on the cover of *Life* magazine, on the September 24, 1971 issue. The cover story was entitled "Rock Stars At Home With Their Parents." *The Jacksons* are shown on a spiral staircase in the den of their Los Angeles home amid "Gold" records, while proud parents Joe and Katherine pose at the bottom of the stairs. Also in the article was Grace Slick of *The Jefferson Airplane*; David Crosby of *Crosby, Stills & Nash*; Elton John; Frank Zappa; and their respective parents. The article read in part:

> *"They have made it very big in a way that is an old story in black America. 'Show business' is still one of the surest routes out of the ghetto. The* Jacksons' *huge new house in Encino, California is testimony to 'Gold' records and sold-out concert*

engagements: swimming pool and basketball court, minibikes, super clothes, toys and other pleasures. Just three years ago their father was a crane operator in Gary, Indiana. 'When the kids were little,' Joseph Jackson says, 'I played guitar with a group called The Falcons. *We would rehearse at the house, and they would be around lookin' up, you know. And from there they tried playing themselves. It wasn't hard to know they could go on to be professionals. They won practically all the talent shows and I wasn't surprised when they did make it. Because, you see we were trying awful hard.'*

So The Jackson Five *is now an institution with a host of spin-offs—fan clubs, a magazine, TV productions. Their father is their manager, and they have a lawyer and an accountant. Because the Five are young, their lives are carefully watched over. The elder Jacksons don't worry about drugs, or outlandish behavior. They are concerned about the difficulties of being 'professionals' at an early age. 'But there is still a part of a child's life that is still a child,' Mr. Jackson says. 'They go to school, do their chores, play ball. They have to maintain their personal lives, because if an entertainer doesn't, that's when he can get the big head. I have tried to teach them to associate with every-body—it doesn't matter what class. Because all people are the same. The only difference is maybe some got a lucky break.' ''*

Well, *The Jackson Five* certainly had gotten their lucky break, and they were riding with it as far as it would take them. For Michael, this fast-paced life was his playground, because he was growing up a media superstar!

Education is always a problem for child stars. It's important for them to receive a proper education without the wasted energy of being a "star" interferring with learning.

"Most of our life we had private schooling," Michael recalls. "I only went to one public school in my life (in Gary). I tried to go to another one here (Los Angeles), but it didn't work, because we'd be in our class and a bunch of fans would break into the classroom, or we'd come out of school and there'd be a bunch of kids waiting to take pictures and stuff like that. We stayed at that school a week. One week! That was all we could take. The rest was private school with other entertainment kids or stars' kids, where you wouldn't have to be hassled."

In 1971, amid their first major tour, *The Jackson Five* was accompanied on the road by a tutor, Mrs. Rose Fine, a Jewish grandmother in her 60's, who found *The Jacksons* to be "fine very nice boys."

"These boys are part of a very tightly-knit family," Mrs. Fine explained, "and they have been raised in an atmosphere of love and discipline. They have an enormous respect for their parents, especially their father, and I think this has kept them from becoming 'little stars.' The parents deserve an awful lot of credit for the job they've done. I've seen too many children turned into egotistical little monsters by this business, but *The Jacksons* are truly exceptions to the rule."

On the road, Bill Bray was *The Jackson Five's* security chief. During this same tour, Bray spoke of his role of acting to ". . . make sure that the boys, especially the young ones, don't get separated in public. For one thing, the boys really dig buying their own clothes. All kids do. We think it's important that the public feel *The Jackson Five* is still accessible, that they're not isolated from the people who helped make them famous. 'J-5' fans feel there's a strong bond between them and the boys and, as long as it doesn't endanger the boys' security, we want to preserve that feeling."

The Christmas season in 1971 found the sixth Jackson Five album under a lot of trees on Christmas morning. In order to give the album something extra, in addition to their previous smashes, this new "Greatest Hits" album was the only LP to contain the group's latest smash "Sugar Daddy." The song sold a million copies, and made it to Number Ten on the Pop charts, and Number Three on the Soul charts in "Billboard" magazine in December.

The Jackson Five finished 1971 as one of the top recording artists in the world. After singing all of the group's biggest hits, what more could Michael do to become more popular, successful, and bigger in the industry, except maybe begin a solo career? And that was exactly what was happening.

4

Michael Jackson Goes Solo

Michael Jackson's solo debut album "Got To Be There," was without a doubt the best Jackson album that had been done to date. Released on January 24, 1972, it was an immediate smash. Again produced by Hal Davis, and The Corporation, it took all of the best aspects of the initial Jackson Five albums, and was arranged to perfectly show off Michael's youthful, but developing voice. Motown President, Berry Gordy Jr. was credited as Executive Producer, and it is evident that he knew that this was the chance to make Michael a full-fledged solo star, without him leaving *The Jackson Five*. It can be viewed as the perfect "two-for-one" stock split. Voilà, two star acts all rolled up into one package, with the added attraction of twice as many record possibilities to capitalize on Jackson-mania!

The album opens with Bill Withers Number One smash "Ain't No Sunshine." Michael even goes Bill

Withers one better. While a guitar whines seductively in the background Michael begins the song with a lamenting soul-bearing soliloquy about his "baby" not sticking around: "Did you ever want something that you know you shouldn't have? The more you know you shouldn't have it, the more you want it. And then one day you get it. And it's *sooo* good to you. But it's just like my girl. When she's around I just feel so good. *Sooo* good. Right now I feel calm. *Sooo* calm, right down to my bones because . . ." and on into the song about being so in love with someone that her absence is next to a world of darkness and pain. Michael sings it to death! Now mind you, this is a thirteen-year-old totally selling a *very* mature love ballad, and pulling it off to a tee! This was the type of performer Michael was then; is it any wonder he continues to astound people with his talent?

The three singles off of the album all hit the nation's "Top Ten" charts. The first single released was the title cut "Got To Be There" and landed in the Number Four spot the last week in October of 1971, preceding the album. The song, an appealing pop ballad, crossed over to both the "Hot 100" chart and the Soul chart with equal appeal. It was the perfect song to be the first Michael Jackson solo single.

The second single was released in December of 1971, and by March of 1972 it was the Number Two song in the country. It was even fresher and more appealing than the one that preceeded it, and even more perfect for Michael to sing . . . it was "Rockin' Robin." It is the only real fast song on the album, and was a treat every time it came on the radio. I'll never forget Spring break that year, and driving from Detroit to Ft. Lauderdale.

Every time the radio station in the car was changed, there would be Michael singing about "Every little swallow, every chickadee," encouraging the "Rockin' Robin" to "go bird go!"

The third single was "I Wanna Be Where You Are," which peaked at Number Two the beginning of June. Both "Got To Be There" and "Rockin' Robin" sold a million copies, and the rest of the album was a hit too.

Also on Michael's debut LP were great versions of Carole King's "You've Got a Friend," which James Taylor had a hit with, and yes, another Supremes song! This time around it was *The Supremes'* "Love Is Here And Now You're Gone."

The "Got To Be There" album is a "must" for every Michael fan, and is currently in re-release by Motown, so if you haven't heard it, by all means do.

It was that winter of 1972 that *The Jackson Five* cartoon show debuted on television. Aired on Saturday mornings, it only intensified the interest in Michael and *The Jackson Five*.

The eighth *Jackson Five* album "Looking Through The Windows" was released on May 17, 1972, and sold a million copies in the United States. This time around Motown was giving more of their stable of producers a hand at this hot quintet in the studio. Hal Davis, who later produced "Love Hangover" for Diana Ross, and "Red Hot" for Mary Wilson, provided this album with "Doctor My Eyes," "Don't Want To See Tomorrow," "Children Of The Light," and the title cut. Johnny Bristol produced "E-Ne-Me-Ne-Mi-Ne-Moe," Willie Hutch produced "I Can Only Give You Love." and Jerry Marcellino & Mel Larson provided "Little Bitty Pretty One," and "Ain't Nothin' Like

The Real Thing.'' The rest of the tunes were done by The Corporation, with Berry Gordy overseeing the project.

The result was a million-selling album. It is one of the most satisfying *Jackson Five* albums ever released, it had a nice hard rock edge on ''Doctor My Eyes,'' lushness on the title tune, and a ''fun'' pop feeling on ''Little Bitty Pretty One.'' In this instance, the diversity of the songs was the key to the album's success.

Both of the American singles reached the ''Top Ten'' charts: ''Little Bitty Pretty One'' was 'Number Eight,' and ''Lookin' Through The Windows'' was Number Five. At this same time *The Jackson Five* had a huge following around the world, and especially in Great Britain. Bill Withers original ''Ain't No Sunshine'' and Jackson Browne's original version of ''Doctor My Eyes'' were American hits that never charted in England, however Michael and *The Jackson Five* respectively made their British singles of these songs smashes on that side of the Atlantic Ocean.

Michael's fourth solo single was released in the spring of 1972, and was the title song to the movie ''Ben.'' It was to become his biggest solo Motown single of the entire decade of the 1970's! The beautiful ballad logged in at the Number One slot of the *Billboard* record charts in August. The movie ''Ben'' was the sequel to the previous summer's hit film ''Willard.'' Both deal with a frustrated young man who learns that he has the power of persuasion over a pack of rats. He uses the rats to seek revenge on those who are making his life miserable. The young man's name is Willard, and his ''main rat'' and best friend is a fuzzy little rodent named Ben. Cute hmmm? The lyrics of the song never mention that Ben has four legs, pink eyes, and a scrawney little tail; but tell of a trusting friendship. The single sold two million copies in the United States alone, despite the fact that it is a beautiful ballad about a boy and his rat. To top it all off, the song "Ben" was nominated for an Academy Award as "Song Of The Year," and won a Golden Globe Award.

The album "Ben," is very good also, and was certified 'Gold.' The LP also contains "cover" versions of *The Temptations'* "My Girl" (written by Smokey Robinson & Ronnie White), Stevie Wonder's "Shoo Be Doo Be Doo Da Day," and *The Stylistics'* "People Make the World Go Round." The title cut was the only single released from the "Ben" album. These producers contributed to this album: Hal Davis, The Corporation, and Marcellino & Larson. The Corporation produced the hit single.

Michael's solo career was going so successfully apart from *The Jackson Five,* that Motown also produced the first Jermaine Jackson album that same year, making three Jackson acts off of one core group. Jermaine scored with two hit singles in 1972: "That's How Love Goes" (#23), and the 'Top Ten' re-make of *The Shep & The Limelights'* classic "Daddy's Home" which peaked on the charts at Number Three.

1972 was without a doubt *The Jackson Five*'s biggest year at Motown with four albums, and eight singles both together and as solo acts. *The Jackson Five* also had another hit single that year, "Corner Of The Sky," which peaked at Number Nine the week of November 11. One of the major events of that year came when *The Jackson Five* received commendations from the United States Senate and House of Representatives for

"Contributions to American Youth," and the consistent positive role-model they were providing to kids of all ages.

"Corner Of The Sky" was the first single off of the 1973 album "Skywriter," and was originally from the Broadway hit "Pippin." The show, which had songs written by Stephen Schwartz (who also wrote "Godspell"), also had Motown Records as a prime financial backer, and they were the owners of the soundtrack album and the publishing rights. They not only had *The Jackson Five* covering this tune from the show, but *The Supremes* (Mary Wilson, Jean Terrell & Lynda Lawrence at that time) had a chart hit with the show's "I Guess I'll Miss The Man" (sung in the show by Jill Clayburgh). To top off that year's "Pippin" fest, Michael recorded the show's "Morning Glow" on his third solo album.

"Skywriter" also contained the 'Top Ten' hit "Hallelujah Day," and a "cover" version of *The Supremes'* hit "Touch." "Skywriter" was the group's ninth album, and featured one of their greatest cover photographs, a sepia-toned print of *The Jackson Five* in World War I aviator's outfits in front of a bi-plane. Unfortunately, the album didn't do too much on the charts, a sign of overexposure for the group.

Likewise, Michael's third solo album, "Music & Me," released in 1973, showed that the "magic" of the formula was beginning to wear thin. His only solo single that year, "With A Child's Heart" made it to Number Fourteen on the Soul charts, and peaked at Number Fifty on the Pop charts in May of that year. Also on that album, Michael sang *The Supremes'* "Johnny Raven," and the theme from the Diana Ross movie "Lady Sings The Blues" entitled "Happy" with music by Michel Legrand and lyrics by Smokey Robinson. The most successful album cut was Michael's re-working of "Too Young." Six different producers had a hand at Michael's "Music & Me" album.

Later that year came the tenth *Jackson Five* album, "Get It Together." This time around Hal Davis produced the whole thing. The title cut is a peppy, funky song that soared up to the Number Two spot on the Soul charts, and the song "Don't Say Good Bye Again" has much the same appeal. Again on this album *The Jackson Five* covers a *Supremes'* song, this time around it's "Reflections," and they also do a *Gladys Knight & The Pips* tune: "You Need Love Like I Do (Don't You);" and *The Temptations'* "Hum Along And Dance." The real surprise on the album was "Dancing Machine."

Released in the fall of 1973, the single "Dancing Machine" lingered on the charts long after the "Get It Together" album had ceased to sell. In fact "Dancing Machine" took twenty weeks to finally meander it's way up the charts to become Number One in March of 1974. To capitalize on this, Motown took eight new and previously un-released Jackson Five songs by various producers, and put them on an album entitled "Dancing Machine," and put the hit single on it as the title cut. The song went on to sell two million copies!

"Dancing Machine" was the only Jackson album of 1974, and aside from the title cut, they also scored with the hits "Whatever You Got, I Want" (Number Three) and "I Am Love (Part I & II)" (which made it to Number Five on the Soul charts).

Now, throughout all of these albums and singles, *The Jackson Five*, together and individually, were told what songs to record, and weren't allowed to play any of their own instrumentals in the studio. Motown owned the majority of the publishing rights on all of the songs that the Jacksons' recorded, and they were not allowed to perform their own compositions. Friction was beginning to develop, because they were getting tired of recording so many other's people's hits from the Motown vaults.

At the time, Joe Jackson, their father and manager was quoted as saying of his sons, "Oh, yes they can write music now. They've written some good songs, they're just not recording them yet. I'd like to make some demonstration recordings of the stuff they've written to see how it sounds on tape."

He also expressed his desire for the boys to branch out. "Michael has done a little bit of acting on different television shows. And Jermaine would really like to have a chance to do a film. I think they'd make very good actors, if they could just get the right parts. It doesn't have to be a whole movie of them. They could just have parts in it. Ever since Michael sang the title tune to 'Ben,' he's wanted to get more things in the movie field."

To further strengthen *The Jackson Five*'s relationship with Berry Gordy and his Motown empire, on December 15, 1973 Jermaine married his daughter, Hazel Gordy. However, artistically, and in a business sense, all was not well.

One of the most significant events of 1974 was the Las Vegas debut of *The Jackson Five*. Opening night on 'The Strip' was Wednesday, April 9, with a run continuing at The MGM Grand until April 23. Comedian/impersonator Frank Gorshin was the opening act, and

The Jackson Five was a critical smash. In the April 13, 1974 issue of *The Los Angeles Times*, critic Robert Hilburn wrote, ''The Jackson Five is a stylish, poised, personable set of performers—just the kind of fresh, talented faces Las Vegas sorely needs.'' One of the highlights of the event was their receiving the ''Key To The City,'' and the importance of reaching still a broader audience than ever before.

To ''Vegas-ize'' their act a touch, they also performed a couple of 'easy listening' standards, which they added to their repertoire: ''By The Time I Get To Phoenix'' and ''Killing Me Softly With His Song.'' At this point in time, eleven-year-old Randy, and the young Jackson sisters, Janet, LaToya and Maureen, had joined their five brothers, to really make the show a ''family act.''

In one of it's issues published in 1974, fan publication, *Right On* magazine ran what they called a ''*Jackson Five* Fact Sheet.'' It published this data ''Just To Hip You To The J-5 Facts, and Keep you Hip . . . Add These To Your List Of Things To Know About Your Favorite Singing Family!'' On the subject of Michael it listed the following:

FULL NAME . . . . *Michael Joseph Jackson*
HEIGHT . . . . *5'5"*
WEIGHT . . . . *128 lbs.*
BIRTHDATE . . . . *August 29, 1958*
ZODIAC SIGN . . . . *Virgo*
BIRTHPLACE . . . . *Gary, Indiana*
PRESENT RESIDENCE . . . *Encino, California*
COLOR OF EYES . . . . *Brown*

The article goes on to list these "fab facts":

1. *One of Michael's favorite pastimes is oil painting.*
2. *Mexican food is one of Michael's favorite foods (especially tacos and enchiladas).*
3. *Michael loves to talk to his friends on the phone.*
4. *Michael prefers performing in concert close to the fans more than on television.*
5. *One of the ways Michael stays so slim is by performing on stage.*
6. *The kind of girl that Michael prefers is a pleasant girl with lots of personality.*
7. *When he was much younger, Michael used to enjoy playing with his two white mice and watching cartoons on T.V.*
8. *Michael was the first member of the J-5 to cut a solo record and album.*

The first of Michael's albums to be released in 1975 was his last original solo Motown album to be recorded. It was entitled "Forever, Michael," and was produced by four different parties: Brian Holland for Holland-Dozier-Holland Productions, Hal Davis, Sam Brown, and Freddie Perren & Fonce Mizell. All in all it is a pretty undistinguishable album. It is mostly mellow, directionless songs that go nowhere musically, however he did have two hit singles off of it. The first single was "We're Almost There," a light ballad that reached Number Seven on the Soul charts and Number Fifty-four on the pop charts. The second single, "Just A Little Bit Of You," which peaked in May of 1975 was a medium-paced song that made it to Number Four on the Soul charts, and Number Twenty-three on the Pop charts. Neither of the songs were bad, but compared to the material that Michael had to his credit at that point, they were highly inferior in emotion and artistry.

After singing new versions of five different Supremes songs ("The Young Folks," "Love Is Here And Now You're Gone," "Touch," "Johnny Raven" and "Reflections") solo and with his brothers; Michael and *The Jackson Five* had a hit with a sixth *Supremes* "cover," which was to become their last 'Top Ten' Motown single. "Forever Came Today" was released at the beginning of the "disco era" and hit Number Six the week of June 28, 1975.

The song was recorded on the twelfth *Jackson Five* album, entitled "Moving Violation." Just like the original Supremes version, "Forever Came Today" was produced by Holland-Dozier-Holland Productions, as was the majority of the "Moving Violation" album. The album also contained the last single released by *The Jackson Five*, "All I Do Is Think Of You," which never made it past Number Fifty on the Soul charts in *Billboard* magazine. "Moving Violation" was the last *Jackson Five* album to be released while the group was still under contract to Motown, although five more albums bearing *The Jackson Five* name eventually appeared as either "greatest hits" packages, or compilations of primarily "out-takes" from previous recording sessions.

Also in 1975, Motown Records released "The Best of Michael Jackson," with ten of his best solo recordings, some singles, some not. Likewise with Michael solo, two more of his albums appeared on Motown, but he was all done recording for the company.

In March of 1976 it was announced that *The Jackson*

Five would not renew it's contract with Motown Records. Since Motown claimed ownership of the trademark name *The Jackson Five*, or *Jackson 5*, in order to leave Motown they had to also leave their name with the record company. Whatever way you slice it, it was the end of *The Jackson Five* and of an era in pop music.

5

"The Jackson Five" Become "The Jacksons"

In March of 1976 when it was decided that *The Jackson Five* was not going to resign their contract with Motown, they left behind not only their name but one of their members as well: Jermaine. *The Jacksons'* father Joe Jackson decided that his boys needed the interest of a new label to continue to grow creatively. Motown never allowed *The Jackson Five* to play their own musical instruments in their recording sessions, they never were allowed to choose their own producers or material, and they could not record their own compositions.

Of all of the offers that Joe Jackson contemplated, CBS Records offered them the best deal. The final decision was made by Joe without consulting his sons.

According to Jermaine, "I came home from fishing with my friend Barry White, and my father called me to

55

come over without Hazel. I knew something was going on. She's a very strong person, and she asks a lot of questions. I'm sure my father thought he could get me to do what he wanted if she wasn't there.''

Jermaine distinctly remembers his confrontation with his father, ''I went to his room and on his bed were the CBS contracts. That was the first I knew about it. That was the wrong way to find out. Because of me being married to Hazel, they thought they couldn't trust me, so they kept me in the dark. Everybody had signed the contract. My father picked up mine and said, 'Sign it.' I said, 'No.' ''

That was the moment the infamous feud began. ''Naturally my brothers thought I betrayed them,'' Jermaine continued. ''So they were mad at me. My father made some crazy statement that it's his blood flowing through my veins and not Berry Gordy's. My mother was asking me what was wrong with me and why did I do what I did. It was a very rough time for me.''

''I was open to talk to them,'' Jermaine explains, ''but I have my pride. They didn't want to talk to me. Why should I keep calling them if they didn't want to talk to me? They didn't understand my reasons. I was nice to them even though they didn't understand me. That's just the way I am. It was tough for me, saying 'no.' It was like I was betraying my family. After that I called up Berry Gordy from this place where I was getting my hair cut. He'd just gotten back from his son's graduation from Beverly Hills High School. I told him my brothers had signed with CBS. He was very quiet and then he said, 'Well, what about you?' and I said, 'Well, my brothers are leaving because they feel

Motown's having problems, but I want to stay and help work out the problems.' That really meant something to him. But I really felt that way even though it meant I was estranged from my brothers and my Dad for a long time after that.''

According to Jermaine, things had changed. "You know, when we first moved out to California, we all lived in one real big house," he says. "Everybody had their own room, their own TV . . . but that house wasn't warm, because everybody would go to their own room and withdraw instead of being together. The house in Gary just had two bedrooms. My parents slept in one, and the rest of us slept in the other. But there was a closeness there, a warmth, that I remember. To me, it's the little things like that that mean so much.

"People said my reason for staying with Motown was that I was married to Berry Gordy's daughter, but it wasn't true. To me it had more to do with loyalty. I believe Motown really cared about us. They groomed us, moved us from Gary to a big home in Hollywood, put us in the best schools, polished us so we'd know how to talk to hosts on talk shows. No other company does that. Actually, I think that way of operating has hurt Motown over the years. They take a personal interest in groups and build them up to be monsters. Then other record companies offer the people more money and they leave, forgetting all the time and effort it took to mold them into successes. But that effort meant something to me. They were willing to invest in us kids in the beginning, and we had hit after hit and sold millions and millions of records.

"But then," he continued, "all of a sudden things were different. Motown was having some problems,

57

and reorganizing their staff, and our records weren't selling like they once did. So my father felt it was time to leave. I thought he should have been closer to Berry Gordy and try to work out things, but he didn't feel that way. Next thing I knew, they were gone."

"It was mainly me who smoothed things over," Jermaine says of the problem he had with his family. He admits, however, that "after a while they were willing to listen. They said I didn't betray them. We all saw that holding grudges is silly. That old thing about time healing all wounds applied here."

However, in 1976, amid the family feud Jermaine remained with Motown Records and signed as a solo artist while his brothers, Michael, Jackie, Tito, Marlon, and Randy signed as *The Jacksons* with the CBS record division known as Epic Records.

"I never regretted my decision," Jermaine admits, "but things were hard for me. It was like they (his family) were trying to rush to outdo me, to prove that I had made the wrong decision by staying, and I really didn't want to sing at all at first. But Berry said that there were a lot of people who still liked me, and I would just have to work really hard to prove what I could do. He was right. And once I started doing things on my own, and gained my brothers respect, they started calling me up and coming around. They stopped talking so much about the breakup."

Jermaine's first solo Motown album since the breakup was entitled "My Name Is Jermaine." The album was produced by various people, and Berry Gordy is credited as Executive Producer. Jermaine had released one single that year, the hit "Let's Be Young Tonight." On the album, if you pay attention to the backgrounds you can hear Thelma Houston lending gospelesque vocal accompaniment. "Let's Be Young Tonight" was a Top Twenty hit for Jermaine.

Meanwhile, at CBS his brothers prepared to go into the studio to record their first album as *The Jacksons*. At that time they reflected about the move they had just made. Said Jackie, "We learned a lot about the music business at Motown. They know how to build a group, how to promote a group, how to put a group on top. We sold a lot of records with them."

"Not only that," Michael added, "but they took care to develop each individual person. Like, Tito likes cars and mechanics, and Jackie likes basketball, and I draw cartoons. With a lot of groups, you know the group's name but you don't know each individual. That was very important to us."

Although they had just left the company, Joe Jackson admitted, "Motown made the group international, and that's very important. There are very big groups in the United States which are not known all over the world as we are."

According to Tito, "Our contract at Motown wasn't up to par compared with other groups of our status at the time, so we felt that it was time for us to either get a better contract or move on. The company that came up with the best deal was CBS. More freedom had a lot to do with it, our own publishing, writing, producing. That's what we were looking for and CBS gave it to us."

As *The Jacksons*, Michael and his brothers' first CBS album was entitled just that, "The Jacksons." The executive producers and album coordinators were the renowned Philadelphia hit-making duo Kenny Gamble &

Leon Huff. Gamble & Huff's biggest hits at that time included "I Love Music" and "Love Train" by *The O'Jays*, "Don't Leave Me This Way" by *Harold Melvin and The Blue Notes*, "I'll Always Love My Mama" by *The Intruders*, "Dirty Ol' Man" by *The Three Degrees*. Since Gamble & Huff had what is known as a "custom label" distributed by CBS known as Philadelphia International Records, the album "The Jacksons" contained both the Epic and Philadelphia International logos, and was certified 'Gold.'

According to Michael, he was excited about working with Gamble & Huff in the studio, "It's a lot of fun working with Kenny Gamble and Leon Huff, they're great producers, and good writers. They know what they're doing. They've proven themselves to be great. Look at all the hits they've had in the past. They go way back. Certain writers have certain styles, it's hard to get away from that, and it seems like they're just mass producing acts, but I don't think they (Gamble & Huff) are. When they wrote the tunes for our album, they went to the mountains in a trailer and stayed for about a week. It was a special project for them!"

Another high point of 1976 was when Michael and his brothers starred in their own successful summer variety series on CBS television. The show entitled "The Jacksons" featured them performing their music and acting in comedy skits with guests including Tim Conway and Redd Foxx.

The Jacksons' first CBS single was the million selling hit "Enjoy Yourself." It became a Number Two hit in October of 1976 and was written by Gamble & Huff, as was the second single "Show You The Way to

Go,'' which became a Number Six hit in April of 1977.

One of the most significant aspects of their first CBS album was the fact that for the first time in their career they had the opportunity to sing their own compositions. Michael wrote the jazzy ballad "Blues Away," and with Tito composed the lush medium tempo "Style of Life." The Jacksons also co-produced both of these cuts along with Gamble & Huff and their associates Gene McFadden, John Whitehead, and Dexter Wansel. (McFadden & Whitehead are best known for their 1979 Number One smash "Ain't No Stoppin' Us Now.")

The second album by *The Jacksons* was released in 1977 and was entitled "Goin' Places." It was again produced by Gamble & Huff and Company. Like the album before it "Goin' Places" also contained two Jackson compositions: "Different Kind Of Lady" and "Do What You Wanna." However, this time the two Jackson songs were produced solely by Michael and his brothers. In this way they were gradually easing into writing and producing their own tunes. Also on this album the brothers were branching out with Tito playing guitar and Randy playing congas on the LP.

One of the high points of 1977 found *The Jacksons* performing for Queen Elizabeth II. As part of Great Britain's Silver Jubilee, they performed in May at Kings Hall, Glasgow, Scotland. In the April 22, 1977 issue of *The New York Post,* an item ran that read, "The group is thrilled about the Royal Command Performance . . . and just sent off copies of their new album to members of the Royal Family so they'll be able to sing along." Yes, it's true, even the Royal Family of England digs Michael Jackson's music!

Two singles were released from this album, the title cut and "Find Me A Girl." "Goin' Places" became a Number Eight hit while "Find Me A Girl" only made it to Number Thirty-eight.

1978 represented a major turning point for *The Jacksons*. For the first time in their long and illustrious career they were responsible for all aspects of their third CBS album aptly entitled "Destiny." It was such a smash that it was certified "Platinum" for sales in excess of one million copies. The first single off of the album was one of Michael's compositions and became a Number Three hit. The second single "Shake Your Body (Down To The Ground)," was written by Michael and Randy and was certified "Platinum" for sales in excess of two million copies.

Michael especially liked the production end of recording "Destiny." "That sound wasn't right for us," he said. "We sounded too much like the other Gamble & Huff artists. I don't like to copy. I like to be original.

"I really enjoy writing songs. It's just another outlet of self-expression that we never had while we were at Motown. We were writing songs then but were never allowed to put them on our albums. It's also nice because most people think all I or my brothers can do is sing and dance, and there's so much more to us. We'd like eventually to get into producing other acts."

Said Tito, "We've been writing all along, songs that we kept in our own personal bank. The first time we introduced our material to the public was when we went to CBS and did our first album. Then there were two on the second album, and now it's all of them!"

On the subject, Marlon added, "We had a lot of

material, more than we could use on this album. We'll use that on the next one.''

Said Jackie, "But we might do something to top that. We did on this album, just kept writing, topping ourselves.''

According to Michael, who really enjoyed writing with his brothers; "It's much easier to write that way. Everybody has a different point of view, and something to add.''

"Also, you have certain mood,'' explained Tito, "You can't just say, 'I'm going to write a song.' and sit down and write it. So, say maybe Jackie and Marlon don't have their heads into what we're trying to get, so Michael and I, or Randy will work on it first.''

Said Marlon of the production experience, "When we were mixing the album, a lot of people thought each one of us would have a knob on the board but we out-slicked all of them. We'd send maybe Tito and Michael in to mix it down, and the rest of us would sit out and wait until they'd get the mix. Then fresh ears would come into listen to it, because you keep hearing the song over and over, you lose something. The next song, somebody else would mix it down.''

After "Destiny'' Michael was confident about their recording process. "I like it, and if I like it, I know they (the record buyers) will! I keep up with the songs and the times. I feel we know what's happening!''

Speaking of the changes that they had gone through since leaving Motown, Michael reflected, "Ever since we started, people close to us were trying to make sure we didn't get big heads. But I don't think I could have been that way even if no one had been watching me. A whole lot of people concentrate on egos and whatever you do they still think you have a big ego. I try to be as nice as possible and some kids still say, 'What's wrong with you, you think you're too good for us.' You try to do things right with some people and it still comes out wrong.

"It's kind of a shame we couldn't grow up doing what the other kids did. We had to rehearse every day after school when the other kids were outside playing. Sometimes we could hear all the fun and excitement outside, but we could never join in. We missed trick-or-treating and football games and all that. Sure, we had plenty of things the other kids didn't have, but we had to sacrifice to get those things."

Here was Michael in 1977, at the age of nineteen, basically spending his teenage years in "a glass bubble." At an age when most kids were living carefree lives and discovering their own independence and finding out what life was all about, Michael was off in his own little world. This accounts for the reason that years later in the 1980's he still has yet to emerge from this over-protected existence.

"I know I am different from most people my age," Michael admits, "because I've seen so much and done so much. I was raised in this business. I've been singing since I was five. But I feel God created certain people to do certain things. We were just chosen to do this. We have talent—and I'm not saying this in a bragging sense, I'm saying this out of rejoice—we were chosen to entertain people!"

The only other people that Michael feels totally comfortable with are his friends who are also in show business. At this time there was a lot of talk about who Michael was dating. In a couple of instances he went out with actress Stephanie Mills who was then starring in the hit Broadway show "The Wiz," and with film actress Tatum O'Neal.

"Well, I guess I am dating her (Tatum O'Neal) in a way. I've taken her out a couple of times—or she's taken me out—whatever. I met her sometime back when Paul McCartney gave a party on the Queen Mary boat. She (Tatum) was there and we talked a little bit. Two years went by before I saw her again, which was at a club on Sunset Boulevard, called 'The Roxy'. We talked and talked and talked. The next day she invited me to join her at Hugh Hefner's house to watch 'Roots' on video tape. She got sort of bored, so we went outside and got into the jacuzzi. We weren't naked, as people have said. We both had on bathingsuits, just enjoying ourselves. And that's it. But she is a friend of mine, and I see her occasionally."

Also in 1977 there were ridiculous rumors circulating about Michael's sex life. One crazy piece of gossip claimed that Michael was going to have a "sex change" operation, and was having a steamy affair with Clifton Davis, the writer of "Never Can Say Goodbye." Michael emphatically denied the allegation in the September 12, 1977 issue of *Soul* magazine. "I was at Caesar's Palace some time ago and Clifton Davis was there, with Leslie Uggams. I was with Diana Ross. I was holding Diana's hand and Clifton was holding Leslie's hand. It would have been the perfect shot for a magazine to take the photos and retouch them so that it would look like Clifton and I were holding hands with each other. Do you believe the magazines have been writing that he and I are getting married? I don't believe it! Clifton came up to me and said, 'Michael! You're not a girl!' I said, 'Man, you're crazy!' He told me he was so mad about the rumors that he's put his lawyers on it. They can track it down by getting with the magazines that talk about it. They don't have to publish that stuff. They know it's not true. I hadn't seen him in ages, and they're saying I 'go' with him. Crazy!

"People make up those things because they have nothing better to do," he continued. "Some people let rumors like that get to them and have nervous breakdowns and stuff like that, but if I let that kind of talk get to me, it would only show how cheap I was. I know it's not true, so it doesn't bother me. I'm sure we must have plenty of fans who are gay, and that doesn't bother me in the slightest, but I'm not gay. I don't know why people say those things.

"My fans are my dates. They're at our gate every day, and I'll go out and sign autographs."

Although the Jackson home has guard dogs, and a tall fence around it, fanatical fans have penetrated the inner sanctum. Michael remembers, "One lady jumped over the gate. She walked into the house and sat down in the den. 'God sent me.' she said. A family drove in and toured the house, and we didn't even know it until our little sister told us because we were all a block away, where we have our recording studio. Fans ask some strange questions. Some don't think you're real. One asked me in front of everybody, 'Do you go to the bathroom?' I was so embarrassed I didn't know what to say.

"Mostly you're never alone. I may want to just go walking or sit in a tree, but everything we do is on TV, or in the newspapers. On tour, with fans hanging around, you can't even go into the hotel lobby so you stay in the room all day. When you're a performer, people want everything. They pull your hair out, break down barricades. People have been crushed at our concerts. Once, at a record shop in San Francisco, over a thousand kids showed up, and they broke the window. A girl's throat was slit, a boy's arm cut. An ambulance took them away and the kids were still grabbing!''

To escape the ill-effects of the pressures of public life Michael concentrated on his spiritual beliefs. ''Science is so silly sometimes,'' explained Michael, ''The sun has been up there for ages and ages—what holds it up? I don't care how many scientific explanations they give me, it ain't deep enough for me. And by travelling the world, I know there must be a God. I've seen so much. I've been in the poorest of homes and the richest of homes. Sometimes I just want to take all the children of the world in my arms . . . really! In the Phillipines and Africa, people are living in cardboard houses. You can watch the wind blow them down. It's sad.''

On the subject of smoking marijuana, Michael denied that he had tried it at that point. ''Never, in my honest-to-God life. I've never tried it,'' he insisted, ''and I don't want to try it. I've been offered it. I'm not interested in it. I'm happy the way I am. I don't even like the word 'high.' If I want to feel free in my mind, I'll go walk the beach, read a beautiful book, or write a song, or spend time with children, which I love to do.''

On stage things had changed for Michael too. ''Ever since we started singing Jermaine was in a certain spot near me onstage. All of a sudden he was gone. It felt bare on that side for a long time. Marlon sings Jermaine's parts now. I'm still getting used to the change.''

In 1976 when the first album by *The Jacksons* was

released, Motown put out their last *Jackson Five* album. It contained all new and previously unreleased material, and was titled ''Joyful Jukebox Music.'' The label read ''The Jackson 5, Featuring Michael Jackson,'' and the title cut is a bouncy pop tune that could have been a hit, but wasn't. The album also contained a lushly orchestrated biographical tune entitled ''We're Here To Entertain You.'' The song begins with Michael singing about himself and his brothers learning to perform before they could walk. The song is one of the album's real highlights. ''Joyful Jukebox Music'' isn't an incredibly great album, but contains some very good *Jackson Five* music, and has become a collector's item.

'' 'Joyful Jukebox Music' never even made the charts,'' Michael commented. ''I don't think Motown promoted it too heavily. We don't feel as limited with Epic. Our music at Motown had to be written by certain people. Producers were another issue. On the album 'Dancing Machine,' we used several producers, but we just wanted to use one. But they wanted us to do it their way, so we came up with a bunch of different sounds on the same record, which happens when a lot of producers are used. That wasn't the best way to do it.''

To eclipse all of their re-packages, also in 1976 Motown released the ultimate *Jackson Five* 'greatest hits' package, *The Jackson Five* ''Anthology,'' a three-record set that traces the group's chart successes from 1969's ''I Want You Back'' to 1975's ''Forever Came Today.'' The six-sided LP has a full-color booklet with it, and covers all phases of *The Jackson Five's* career, including the solo hits by Michael and Jermaine. ''Anthology'' was the fourteenth *Jackson Five* album released on Motown.

"I see myself as a ballad singer," Michael explained at the time of that record's release. "I like fast songs too but I like ballads much better. I see a whole new thing opening up for me." With regard to his high visibility within the group he continued, "I sing up front and more people know my name because I'm up front and they want to know who that person is. Motown decided to take a chance on me with the solo albums. It's up to the public. It's like a vote, they decide to pick you. We've travelled around the world, and if we don't sing 'Ben' they all go crazy. I could never believe how big that song was. I haven't done a solo album in a long time but I will be doing some more."

6

"The Wiz"

"I like the idea of doing 'The Wiz,' " exclaimed Michael in the summer of 1977, "because it has the best people working in it. When you're working with the best in anything, you know it's going to come out right. Sidney Lumet is the director. He's one of the hottest directors around—'Network,' 'Day of the Condor'—he's done some good stuff. Quincy (Jones) is doing the music—it should be great. And it's got Richard Pryor, Diana Ross, Mabel King. How can it lose?"

"Anybody can act," said Michael at the time. "I've never really tried it seriously, just joking around, like on the T.V. show we had. On T.V. I never had any real time to study anything, we just had to do it. Quick! With the movie, you go over the lines over and over again. That's why it'll take so long to film. It's got to be right. I'm playing the Scarecrow, which is dancing and singing—I can do it."

As early as 1971, Michael had confessed to Michael Sherman of *The Detroit Free Press*, that he had motion picture asperations. "I'd like to be an actor," said Jackson, "like the kind of things Sidney Portier does." And now he was about to have his chance, playing a scarecrow who looks to the newspaper clippings his head is stuffed with for ideas.

Not only was the motion picture version of the smash Broadway production "The Wiz" the most expensive Black film ever produced, with a budget in excess of $30 million, it was the most costly movie musical ever filmed in the history of Hollywood!

Michael's co-stars were to include Diana Ross as Dorothy, Ted Ross as The Cowardly Lion, Nipsey Russell as The Tin Man, Mabel King as the wicked witch Evilene, Richard Pryor as The Wiz, and the legendary Lena Horne as Glinda the good witch.

The original concept of Broadway's "The Wiz" began in the mind of producer Ken Harper. In 1972, Harper was a thirty-two-year-old ex-disc jockey with a blossoming idea that a musical with Motown-type music would have the same universal appeal, on the stage as it did pouring out of radio speakers. With William Brown's book and Charlie Small's score and lyrics, "The Wiz" was born.

The next task was to get someone equally enthused about the project—enough to invest a largest sum of money to get the show on the road. After phoning every lead that he could possibly think of, Harper finally touched home base with an interested Twentieth Century Fox. Fox was enthralled, and in exchange for the first option on film rights, publishing rights and album rights, fronted the initial $650,000. The project was on its way to the top.

Harper wasted no time gathering together the winning team of actors and technicians, especially Stephanie Mills to play Dorothy, and Geoffrey Holder (who is probably best recognized for the role which won him the advertising industry's Clio Award for a 7-Up commercial "These are *Cola Nuts*"), to do the costumes and, eventually, the directing.

Finally, slated to open in Baltimore at the Morris A. Mechanic Theatre on October 21, 1974, the night before the premiere performance, the technical rehearsal was an absolute disaster and Harper had visions of his three-year dream going up in smoke. The theater is still one of the most superstition-oriented organizations around, and as per tradition, if your dress rehearsal is a mess, opening night somehow pulls together. Following that same theory, the first performance was met with a standing ovation and four curtain calls, while subsequent out-of-town boosters were drawn from adulating audiences in Detroit and Philadelphia.

New York, however, was another story. After a week's worth of previews, the show was drowning in expenses. With a cost of $67,000 per week to put the show on, previews grossed only $46,000. On Saturday, January 5, 1975, their Broadway opening night, a closing notice was posted. When the reviews came out they were described as "mixed," but tended to be somewhat negative.

Harper knew that he had a good show comprised of many excellent elements; but the money was gone, and if Fox hadn't lost faith at that point—the reviews would probably have killed it. On Monday the word came through . . . Fox would grant the necessary funds to float the show another month—but there had to be marked sales improvement or that would be the end. Evidently, the movie company that laughed all the way to the bank when the critics slaughtered ''The Poseidon Adventure,'' was willing to gamble once again.

The Broadway musical went on to be the season's biggest Tony Award-winner. It not only won the 1975 Tony Award for ''Musical of the Year,'' it continued to run on Broadway for nearly four years. What an excellent idea for a film!

The first person to conceive of the movie version of ''The Wiz'' was producer Rob Cohen. The initial person he thought of enlisting was award-winning director Sidney Lumet. Lumet loved the idea, but realized that the film would only be as strong as it's musical director. He decided immediately that there was just one man for the task: Academy Award nominee Quincy Jones.

Sidney Lumet recalls, ''When I first called Quincy to come work on 'The Wiz,' he didn't know if he'd be able to do it. He had four albums to do that year. I was stunned. I literally didn't know which way to look because the combination of talent needed to fulfill what I saw was so enormous that there was only one person to fill that vacuum.''

''When in doubt, lie still. I postponed all decisions. I figured we'd do our pre-records with the best rhythm section we could put together, and then when shooting was over, I'd pray alot.''

Continues Lumet, ''Once Quincy and I had talked, however, he couldn't stay away. I'll never know how he worked it out, and I'm not sure I want to. But as you listen to this, you'll be, as I am, just deeply grateful that he did work it out.

"What was it that made the job so specifically one that only Quincy could fill? There was Charlie Small's lovely score from the play that, from what I felt for the movie version, had been still untouched. There would be the necessity of four new songs, two ballads and two rousers, that I knew only Quincy could write.

"I had to have someone who could understand what we were reaching for in L. Frank Baum's classic; who could understand why one set was this color and another set that color; who could talk to a choreographer and just look at a rough marking of a dance number and know what was intended; who could watch Diana or Michael rehearse a "book" scene and know what musical arrangement the dramatic scene dictated for the song . . . in other words, Quincy Jones."

According to Jones, "For many years people have been asking me, 'Quincy, what was your very first big assignment?' My answer now is 'The Wiz'—Anytime you have nine singing principals, one hundred and twenty dancers, six sound technicians, three conductors, four contractors, three hundred musicians, one hundred and five singers, nine orchestrators, six copyists, five music editors; you're talking big numbers. And to think I came *this* close to not taking it!

"I first heard about the film version of 'The Wiz' from Sidney Lumet at a party two years ago (1976), but I was so tied-up with record commitments that I couldn't consider it. Then one day, a Mercedes pulled up to my home in California, and a man got out with flowers. It was Charlie Small asking me to do the film. I still had to say 'no,' but neither Charlie nor Sidney seemed to hear me. But I've learned through the years that when Sidney is turned on about something that much, 'you sure better check it out!' "

Quincy went on to say, "Dissolve to Rob Cohen, our twenty-nine-year-old producer, a beautiful Pisces person whom I love, and thank for not taking 'no' as an answer. He's the one that started this ball rolling towards the screen after seeing the original Broadway version while he was filming 'Bingo Long and The Travelling All-Stars.' Rob proceeded to put his vision in action by securing the rights to do 'The Wiz,' as a movie musical. First, he signed Ted Ross and Mabel King (from the original cast). Then, in the midst of this preparation, Diana Ross had a dream about being Dorothy and 'look out!' Rob, then set his sights on Richard Pryor and Michael Jackson. He pulled the master stroke of choosing Sidney Lumet to direct the film and 'The Wiz' was on the way."

Although Twentieth Century Fox had the first option on the film, the rights changed hands and "The Wiz" became a Motown Production and a film for Universal Pictures. Motown and MCA shared in the recording rights, but it was MCA that was in charge of the distribution.

While the majority of the film was shot at Astoria Studios in Queens, Quincy distinctively remembers, "Rehearsals started July 1977 at the St. George Hotel in Brooklyn. Sidney worked in one small room with the actors on the script. While Louis Johnson worked in the main ballroom with one hundred-twenty dancers and forty top New York black fashion models. What a sight! What a birth!'

"What a cast! What a diversity of styles. From Lena

Horne to Diana Ross to Richard Pryor to Ted Ross to Michael Jackson (who just turned nineteen). Each artist had his own working way!'' exclaims Jones. And so began the first working creative collaboration between Quincy Jones and Michael Jackson.

All of the actors were very excited about the fantasy roles they were about to portray. Each of them carefully studied L. Frank Baum's original 1902 classic ''The Wonderful Wizard of Oz.''

Said Michael Jackson at the time, ''Like all of the characters in 'The Wiz,' I'm a prisoner of myself. I'm afraid to fulfill my potential. I rely on my clippings rather than to think with the brains I really have.''

''This Lion is a bookworm,'' explained Ted Ross of his character. ''He's been drummed out of the jungle and this is the only work he can get, sitting on a pedestal,'' he says, explaining The Cowardly Lion's job as a statue on the steps of The New York Public Library.

Nipsey Russell, as The Tin Man, had long been a well-known television personality who was rarely seen on the screen. He exclaimed at the time '' 'The Wiz' is a chance that hasn't come too late! But I'm going to help make this picture too, it's not just the other way around. I've worked hard and I know I'm good at singing and dancing and telling jokes.''

The most controversial casting was indeed the film's most 'bankable' star, Diana Ross. Although it is commonly believed that Dorothy is a young, teen-aged girl from Kansas, Diana found no mention of specific age in the book. ''It's all left imprecise,'' she explained, ''That way, each reader could see it the way he or she wanted. I knew then that my long dream could be a reality.

Dorothy worked on my subconscious. My first trip to Oz was with Judy (Garland.) But it was my own story too. I was the little girl who was afraid to leave home and then found the power I needed within myself.''

To get around the obvious age differential, the script was re-written so that Dorothy became a twenty-four-year-old school teacher. Ross, however, was thirty-four-years-old at the time.

For Michael Jackson the project represented fulfillment of a life-long ambition. ''Doing 'The Wiz' was an incredible experience. It was always something I wanted to do, because I had always loved the movie, and always fell in love with The Scarecrow. I saw the play six times.''

However, before principal filming began, Michael had a real physical health scare. As he tells it, ''I had a lung attack on the beach on the Fourth Of July. I couldn't breathe. They had to rush me to the emergency hospital. The doctor said it was pneumothorax; bubbles on the lungs, and the bubbles burst and you can't breathe. Mostly slim people have it, the doctor said. He said there was a little bit of pleurisy there too. It reminded me that Buddy Ebsen was supposed to be the Tin Man in the original 'Wizard Of Oz,' and he broke down sick before the thing.''

At the time Michael was very thin, so that didn't help his stamina. Weighing only one hundred and fifteen pounds he claimed, ''I eat all the bread off the table to gain weight. I try and nothing happens.'' But like the real trouper he is, he reported to the set on time, and filming went ahead as scheduled.

When Michael began the film, he had no idea how much work actually went into motion pictures. ''I spent four hours a day for five months getting made-up, and it was well worth every minute. Man, that was painful,'' says Jackson. ''I'd finish a day's shooting in all that stuff, and then I'd leave the set with my skin all blotched and marked, and my eyes red and sore. There'd be fans outside and they'd point at me and say, 'Hey, that guy's on drugs—look what it's doing to him!' I'd explain that I never touch drugs, that it was just the make-up for the movie, but I don't think they believed me. Sometimes I would go home in costume and make-up and the people would say, 'Trick or treat!' That was beautiful!''

There were also environmental hazards. Michael recalls, ''we worked outside a lot; it was cold, the coldest ever in New York. There were six hundred dancers at The World Trade Center, all wearing costumes like swim outfits, and it was so cold a lot of them quit.''

Admits Michael, ''I owe a lot to Diana Ross. She was my 'Mama' on the set. I mean it. She was always there, helping me . . . giving me advice. We were really close. I have to say I love her; she was terrific. Every morning she would come to my dressing room and ask 'Are you okay? You need anything?' ''

''The funniest thing,'' he remembers, ''was a scene we were doing on a rooftop. Diana was supposed to faint, and I had to pick her up. But she was too heavy. I kept puffing away on the dialogue while I tried over and over again to lift her, until I finally made it. It wasn't at all funny in another scene, where The Wiz looked our way. They made his eyes so bright, like spotlights, that when Diana looked into them, they burned her retinas. She couldn't see for two days!'' To this day

Diana suffers from retina damage and cannot have cameras' flashes aimed directly into her eyes.

Michael worked very hard and made many friends during the filming. Director, Sidney Lumet, found Michael to be "the most talented young person to come along since Jimmy Dean—a brilliant actor, a phenomenal dancer, one of the rarest talents I've ever worked with! That's no hype!" Says Quincy Jones, "Michael's a truth machine. He's got a balance between the wisdom of a sixty-year-old and the enthusiasm of a child."

Continues Michael of his experience, "I enjoyed it to death. It was one of the most wonderful times I've ever had. I went crazy. I learned so much. It was a wonderful experience. It was a heavy script, real heavy. A lot of people look at it as just a children's story, but it isn't. It's dealing with faith and belief and courage, and when you deal with those subjects you're dealing with things that make kings of the world. Courage and belief and heart—those are heavy things. I just enjoyed it so much!"

In the final analysis, he was very proud of the work he had done. "I'm really pretty happy with what I did; I recognize it as part of the whole thing, and yes, I think it was good. It's really wonderful to know that something you've done, something you've been a real part of, will be around for just years and years. It's funny, too, but my favorite song from the movie isn't one of mine. It's the one that Diana and Lena Horne do. It's called 'Believe in Yourself.' And it's my favorite because of what it says. I like what it says."

He also found the experience to be very educational. "I learned so much from Sidney Lumet. We talked about everything. He knows so much. I was asking him questions about all his films—'Serpico' and 'Dog Day Afternoon' and 'Twelve Angry Men'—I haven't seen that one. Sidney's real good. Sometimes when what I did just wasn't real, I would stop and say, 'Let's do that over!' and Sidney would say, 'No, that's terrific!' ''

With a cast and crew that included Lena Horne, Diana Ross, Richard Pryor, Sidney Lumet, Quincy Jones, Nipsey Russell, *and* Michael Jackson, 'The Wiz' promised to be one of the hottest cinematic experiences ever captured on film. To top it all off, Quincy assembled an incredible group of musicians including Bob James, Grady Tate, Ralph MacDonald, Eric Gale, Richard Tee and Steve Gadd. To sing the choral parts he enlisted such singing greats as Roberta Flack, Cissy Houston, Luther Vandross, Ray Simpson of The Village People, and Ullanda McCullough. For additional music and lyrics he turned to the talents of Nick Ashford and Valerie Simpson. How could it not be one of the biggest hits in movie history? Simple, it was over-produced.

It was so busy and cluttered that the spirit and joy of the story was buried alive. What should have been the biggest smashes of the 1978 Christmas season was an entertaining event that totally lacked the sparkle that made the stage version of ''The Wiz'' a moving experience.

John Skow of *Time* magazine reviewed the film in the October 30, 1978 issue, and titled it ''Nowhere Over The Rainbow.'' Andrew Sarris of *The Village Voice* titled his critique ''Ding Dong, The Wiz Is Dead.'' Critics around the country denounced the film for suffocating in it's own lavishness. Regardless, initial box office grosses were respectable, but it wasn't a film that people have a passion to see over and over again.

Despite the criticisms, however, "The Wiz" was an important step for Michael. He received consistently favorable reviews and was introduced to the movie-going public. His acting was handled professionally and believeably, and he virtually proved himself "bankable" as a movie star.

Even more significantly was the fact that this project created the first album featuring Michael produced by Quincy Jones. This was a union that was later to create "Off The Wall," and "Thriller!" This was the project that made the name of "Michael Jackson" more than just another recording artist, he was now a respected actor as well!

According to Michael, the movie also increased his status within the Hollywood community, particularly with Tatum O'Neal and her actor father, Ryan O'Neal. "Tatum is just about my best buddy. We're always in touch, talking about things to do together. She was really excited for me when I was cast for 'The Wiz.' She helped me too, with advice on how to stay cool through it all. She and her dad have been just great for me."

Recalls Michael proudly, "This is my first *acting* role. I mean, I've been in movies before, but they were concert-type films like 'Save The Children.' This is the first time I played a part instead of just being myself . . . it was one of my dreams that came true!"

Two of Michael's songs in the movie were released as singles. The first one, "Ease On Down The Road," is the only duet recorded to date with Michael and his close friend Diana Ross. It made it to Number Seventeen on the *Billboard* Soul charts in October of 1978. The second single was Michael's only "Wiz" solo song, "You Can't Win (Part 1)" which hit Number Forty-two in January of 1979.

Dorothy was granted her greatest wish by clicking the heels of her "ruby slippers" together. If Michael were able to do the same, what is it he would ask for?

"I would wish to make the world more beautiful by entertaining, to bring joy into people's hearts. It's terrific to see people smile, or laugh or cry with joy. Music, peace, love; that's what I'd wish for!"

7

Michael Goes "Off The Wall"

For Michael Jackson, the year 1979 began with *The Jackson's* 1979 World Tour. Commencing on January 22 in Bremen, Germany, the sojourn concluded in the city of Nairobi, Kenya in Africa. The tour also encompassed Madrid, Amsterdam, Geneva, London, Brighton, Preston, Sheffield, Geneva, Glasgow, Manchester, Birmingham, Halifax, Leicester, Cardiff, Bournemouth, and Paris engagements.

At the time Jackie Jackson said, "I can't think of a better way of starting our anniversary year than meeting our millions of fans all around the world."

"The fellows are really looking forward to returning to London, where the fans are unbelievably exuberant," Michael's father added.

It had been four years since Michael had a solo album released, and by 1979, he was getting anxious to resume his solo recording career. "I want to show that I can make it on my own,'' he exclaimed, ''that my talent doesn't depend on anyone else. I have a responsibility to myself to do that. I guess every kid feels that way.''

He was especially anxious to sing the kind of ballads that can't be sung by a group. ''Songs I do with the group are different from what I sing as a solo artist. I love ballads. A funky rock and roll song can be 'Number One' for three weeks, then you won't hear anything about it. A good ballad—'Mona Lisa,' 'Moon River' —will last forever. On my own album I can do some things I can't do on *The Jacksons'* albums. I can do the ballads I want, I can do whatever I want. I can be different and it's nice to have something to do and to look forward to that's different. It keeps me from getting too crazy.''

Michael was preparing to act ''crazy like a fox,'' as the old addage for clever moves goes. He was about to hit upon his biggest achievement to date.

This was going to be the first time that Michael was totally in the driver's seat for his own solo album. Since he had proven himself a songwriter, and a producer with his brothers on ''Destiny,'' he could virtually do as he pleased. The first big question was who would produce the album, and it was up to Michael to decide. He remembers his delimma in chosing an outside producer. ''After we finished 'The Wiz,' I called Quincy Jones to ask if he knew of any great producers for my album. He started thinking and said, 'I'll tell you what . . . why don't you let me do it?' Boy, was I excited. I never expected Quincy to produce my album, because he's so busy and in such demand. But I'm really grateful that he decided to do it!''

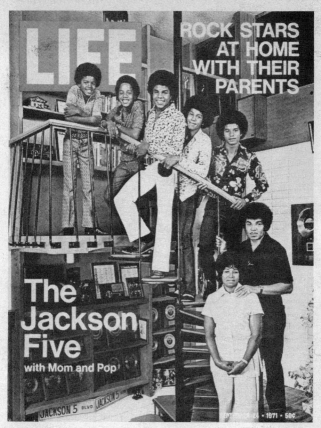

MICHAEL and The Jackson Five on the cover of *Life* magazine, September 24, 1971. (left to right): Michael, Marlon, Jackie, Jermaine and Tito with their parents Joe and Katherine Jackson. (*photo: John Olson for Time Inc.*)

A superstar at the age of 12, MICHAEL JACKSON amid his mountains of fan mail in 1972. (*photo: Wide World*)

MICHAEL JACKSON and the star of the original Broadway version of ''The Wiz,'' STEPHANIE MILLS, June 1977. (*photo: Robin Platzer*)

STEPHANIE MILLS and MICHAEL, June 1977. (*photo: Robin Platzer*)

MICHAEL JACKSON with Aerosmith's STEVEN TYLER and girlfriend DORRIE at the party for ''Beatlemania'' at Studio 54, June 20, 1977. (*photo: Robin Platzer*)

LaTOYA, JANET, and MICHAEL JACKSON at Studio 54, August 1977. (*photo: Robin Platzer*)

MICHAEL gets down on the floor at Studio 54 in New York City, August 1977. (*photo: Robin Platzer*)

MICHAEL with sister LaTOYA JACKSON (right) at Studio 54,
August 1977. (*photo: Robin Platzer*)

MICHAEL with dancers from ''The Wiz,'' at a party in his honor at
Studio 54, October 25, 1977. (*photo: Robin Platzer*)

MICHAEL boogies with dancers from ''The Wiz,'' at Studio 54, October 25, 1977. (*photos: Robin Platzer*)

THE JACKSONS: RANDY, MICHAEL, TITO, JACKIE and MARLON at Studio 54, October of 1977. (*photo: Robin Platzer*)

MARILYN McCOO and BILLY DAVIS JR. with MICHAEL at Studio 54, October 1977. (*photo: Robin Platzer*)

TITO, MICHAEL, JACKIE and RANDY JACKSON at "The First Annual Rock 'N' Roll Sports Classic," March 10, 1978. (*photo: Robin Platzer*)

MICHAEL on the sidelines at "The First Annual Rock 'N' Roll Sports Classic," March 10, 1978. (*photo: Russell C. Turiak*)

ANDREA McARDLE of Broadway's ''Annie,'' and MICHAEL JACK-SON in 1978. (*photo: Russell Turiak*)

MICHAEL JACKSON in Central Park, New York City, October 1978. (*photo: Robin Platzer*)

MICHAEL relaxes in a tree in New York City's Central Park, October of 1978. (*photo: Robin Platzer*)

MICHAEL and his radio in Central Park, October 1978. (*photo: Robin Platzer*)

MICHAEL out on a limb, in Central Park, October 1978. (*photo: Robin Platzer*)

MICHAEL swings in Central Park, October 1978. (*photo: Robin Platzer*)

MICHAEL makes friends with a stuffed St. Bernard in Manhattan's famed toy store, F.A.O. Schwartz, October 23, 1978. (*photo: Robin Platzer*)

LENA HORNE, MICHAEL, and director SIDNEY LUMET at the opening night party for ''The Wiz,'' October 1978. (*photo: Robin Platzer*)

NIPSEY RUSSELL, GLORIA SWANSON and MICHAEL at a party for ''The Wiz,'' October of 1978. (*photo: Russell Turiak*)

BEN VEREEN, CICELY TYSON and MICHAEL JACKSON at a party, 1978. (*photo: Russell Turiak*)

MICHAEL with MARGAUEX HEMMINGWAY at a party in 1978. (*photo: Russell Turiak*)

MICHAEL celebrates his birthday at Studio 54, August of 1979.
(*photo: Russell Turiak*)

MICHAEL receiving his ''Platinum'' album for ''Off The Wall'' from JANE FONDA, 1979. (*photo: Epic Records*)

MICHAEL surrounded by BRUCE JENNER, THE VILLAGE PEOPLE: (construction worker DAVID HODO, cowboy RANDY JONES, leather man GLENN HUGHES, cop RAY SIMPSON, soldier ALEX BRILEY, Indian FELIPE ROSE); VALERIE PERRINE (left) and JANE FONDA (right) at Jane's Halloween disco party at The Hollywood Palace 1979. (*photo:Wide World Photos*)

JOHN TRAVOLTA with MICHAEL at a party, 1980. (*photo: Epic Records*)

DIANA ROSS and MICHAEL at The American Music Awards in L.A. January 30, 1981. (*photo: Ron Galella*)

DIANA ROSS and MICHAEL at The American Music Awards in L.A. January 30, 1981. (*photo: Ron Galella*)

MICHAEL JACKSON / May 1981 (*photo: Matthew Rolston for Epic Records*)

KATHARINE HEPBURN, MICHAEL, KATHARINE HOUGHTON (Ms. Hepburn's niece and star of ''Guess Who's Coming To Dinner''), and JACKIE JACKSON, backstage at Madison Square Garden, August 1981. (*photo: Epic Records*)

MICHAEL JACKSON / December 1982 (*photo: Epic Records*)

Michael Jackson / January 1983 (*photo: Epic Records*)

MICHAEL JACKSON and JANE FONDA exchange ''Platinum'' albums February 25, 1983. Michael's ''Thriller'' album went ''Double Platinum,'' while Jane's ''Workout'' went ''Platinum'' that month. (*photo: Janet Gough for California Features*)

MICHAEL JACKSON at the CBS Records press conference where he was presented with his ''Double Platinum'' certification for ''Thriller,'' February 25, 1983. (*photo: Janet Gough for California Features*)

MICHAEL JACKSON in Los Angeles amid the taping of the video of "Beat It," March 9, 1983. (*photo: Barry King for California Features*)

JENNIFER HOLLIDAY, star of "Dreamgirls" at the L.A. opening night party with MICHAEL, March 20, 1983. (*photo: Janet Gough for California Features*)

REX SMITH, LINDA LEILAHNE BROWN of the L.A. cast of "Dreamgirls," and MICHAEL at the opening night party for "Dreamgirls," March 20, 1983. (*photo: Janet Gough for California Features*)

OLIVIA NEWTON-JOHN with MICHAEL at the "Dreamgirls" party, March 20, 1983. (*photo: Janet Gough for California Features*)

"Dreamgirls" stars DEBORAH BURRELL (left) and LINDA LELAHNE BROWN (right) with MICHAEL at the opening night party for the show, March 20, 1983. (*photo: Janet Gough for California Features*)

MICHAEL at the "Dreamgirls" L.A. opening night party, March 20, 1983. (*photo: Janet Gough for California Features*)

The six Jackson brothers re-united at Pasadena Civic Auditorium for the "Motown 25" rehearsal, March 25, 1983. MICHAEL with his hands in the air in the center. (*photo: Russell Turiak*)

RANDY, MARLON, MICHAEL, and JACKIE JACKSON leave the "Motown 25" rehearsal, March 25, 1983. (*photo: Russell Turiak*)

RANDY JACKSON and his brother MICHAEL at The Pasadena Civic Auditorium for ''Motown 25,'' March 25, 1983. (*photo: Russell Turiak*)

MICHAEL backstage at Pasadena Civic Auditorium at the taping of the TV special ''Motown 25: Yesterday, Today, Forever,'' March 25, 1983. (*photo: Janet Gough for California Features*)

MICHAEL at the ''Motown 25'' party, March 25, 1983. (*photo: Russell Turiak*)

QUINCY JONES, MICHAEL JACKSON and DAVID GEFFEN (president of Geffen Records) at a post-concert party for Liza Minnelli, at The New Universal Amphitheatre in Hollywood, April 6, 1983. (*photo: Brad Elterman for California Features*)

LIZA MINELLI gets a big hug from MICHAEL at her post-concert party, April 6, 1983. (*photo: Brad Elterman for California Features*)

MICHAEL and actor SAMIR KAMOUN pay tribute to Charlie Chaplin on the anniversary of Chaplin's birth: April 16, 1983. (*photo: Epic Records*)

Author MARK BEGO interviewing JOHN "JELLYBEAN" BENITEZ at Kennedy Airport, October 2, 1983. Benitez remixed the Michael Jackson/Paul McCartney duet "Say, Say, Say." (*photo: David Salidor*)

''He just has so much creativity!'' says Supreme MARY WILSON of Michael. (*photo: Marc Raboy*)

MICHAEL JACKSON / August 1983 (*photo: Matthew Rolston for Epic Records*) This outfit was styled by Jill Klein. Note: the four antique pins that she assembled for this ''princely'' look.

Quincy recalls that he was pleasantly surprised by Michael while working with him on "The Wiz." "I saw another side," he says. "Watching him in the context of being an actor, I saw a lot of things about him as a singer that rang a lot of bells. I saw a depth that was never apparent, and a commitment. I saw that Michael was growing up."

The next task was selecting material, which Michael and Quincy both worked on. One of the most notable events of the recording was that it marked the first time Michael worked with Paul McCartney. "The McCartney thing came about when I got invited to a party at his house," Michael explains. "I met Linda McCartney first, and after we said 'Hi!' she told me that they had written a song for me. That was 'Girlfriend,' and they just started singing to me right there on the spot. They gave me their Scotland number and their England number. But I called them the next day in Beverly Hills and we got it together right away for the 'Off The Wall' album."

Michael wrote three songs for the album, "Don't Stop 'Til You Get Enough," "Working Day And Night," and "Get On The Floor" (co-written by Louis Johnson of *The Brothers Johnson*). Stevie Wonder and former Supreme Susaye Greene wrote "I Can't Help It," Carole Bayer Sager and David Foster composed "It's The Falling In Love," Tom Bahler penned "She's Out Of My Life," and Red Temperton wrote "Rock With You," "Burn This Disco Out," and the title song "Off The Wall."

Michael was very happy with his association with Quincy, and with the outcome. "I listen to the album all the time! Working with Quincy was really great. He's wonderful in how he deals with you. He's not selfish in the studio. In other words, he wants you to share your ideas.'' Michael and Quincy co-produced three of the songs: "Don't Stop 'Til You Get Enough," "Working Day And Night," and "Get On The Floor."

Jones recalls one particular experience with Michael, "I had a song I'd been saving for Michael called 'She's Out Of My Life.' Michael heard it, and it clicked. But when he sang it, he would cry. Every time we did it, I'd look up at the end and Michael would be crying. I said, 'We'll come back in two weeks and do it again, and maybe it won't tear you up so much.' Come back, and he started to get teary. So we left it in."

The first single off of the album was "Don't Stop 'Til You Get Enough," and it was released in July of 1979. It was a long steep climb, but it wasn't long before it was the Number One song in the country. It was followed by the Number One smash "Rock With You," which was at the top of the charts the first week of January in *Billboard*, *Record World*, and *Cash Box* magazines, making it the first Number One song of the decade of the 1980's. Not a bad way for Michael to begin the '80's!

That same month ABC-TV's "20/20" proclaimed *The Jacksons* (solo, as a group, and as *The Jackson Five*), the largest selling rock group, after *The Beatles*. Michael and *The Jacksons* had by then racked up a sales figure in excess of ninety-three million records sold worldwide! As Stevie Wonder so brilliantly put it, "It has taken some people quite a few years and millions of pop hit records to realize what I knew and felt from the very beginning. *The Jacksons* have been, and continue to be, the most talented family in the history of show business."

On the television special, The American Music Awards, telecast January 18, 1980, Michael Jackson tied Donna Summer for the most awards, at three apiece. Michael won in the Soul category, "Favorite Male Vocalist," "Favorite Album" for "Off The Wall," and "Favorite Single" for "Don't Stop 'Til You Get Enough."

When the third and fourth singles off of the album ("Off The Wall" and "She's Out Of My Life") both hit the "Top Ten," the "Off The Wall" album made musical history—it was the first solo record album to have four "Top Ten" hits. Each of the four singles were certified "Gold" for sales in excess of a million copies. Michael went on to win a Grammy Award for "Best Male R&B Vocal Performance" for "Don't Stop 'Til You Get Enough."

The album sold five million copies in the United States, and eight million worldwide. In England the LP was certified "Triple Platinum," in Australia it was seven times "Platinum," in Canada it was "Triple Platinum," and in Holland it was certified "Gold." The album spent nearly eight months in *Billboard* magazine's "Top Ten," and spent a consecutive eighty-four weeks on that publication's charts. In England, the song "Girlfriend" was also released as a single, setting another record, as it was the first time that five chart singles in that country came from the same LP. Suddenly, Michael Jackson was the hottest male recording artist in the world!

To add to the 1980's continuing "Jackson-mania," Michael and *The Jacksons* released their fourth CBS studio album, entitled "Triumph," it was again entirely written and produced by themselves. It contained four hits, "Lovely One," "Heartbreak Hotel," "Can You Feel It," and "Walk Right Now," and was certified "Platinum."

On both the "Triumph" and "Destiny" albums, the back of the jacket displays large colorful peacocks. On the "Triumph" album, Michael wrote the following inscription explaining the beautiful bird's appearance: "Through the ages, the peacock has been honored and praised for its attractive, illustrious beauty. In all the bird family, the peacock is the only species that integrates all colors into one, and displays this radiance of fire only when in love. We, like the peacock, try to integrate all races into one, through the love and power of music." *The Jacksons'* continuous universal appeal attests to their accomplishing this goal.

Also in 1980, The Hollywood Chamber Of Commerce, saluted *The Jacksons'* contributions to the entertainment field, and presented the group with their own "star" along Hollywood Boulevard's historic "Walk Of Fame." A crowd of over two-thousand fans lined the streets for this historic event.

To capitalize on the resurgence of interest in Michael Jackson, and *The Jacksons,* from 1979-1981, Motown eleased two albums by Michael, and two albums by *The Jackson Five.* 1979 saw the appearance of *The Jackson Five*'s album "Boogie." This one is a real collector's item, as it contains seven previously-unreleased cuts by the original group, and very few copies were pressed. It was released on the Motown label called "Natural Resources" which was used for about two years, and then disbanded. The seven rare songs on this album are "Love's Gone Bad," "I Ain't Gonna Eat Out My Heart Anymore," the Stevie Wonder hit "I

Was Made To Love Her," "One Day I'll Marry You," "Oh, I've Been Bless'd," "Penny Arcade," and "Just Because I Love You." To round out the package, "ABC," "Never Can Say Goodbye," and "Dancing Machine" were included. On many of the new cuts on "Boogie," Michael's voice is shown off as much more raw and funky than on many of the familiar selections on other *Jackson Five* albums. "Love's Gone Bad," and "Ain't Gonna Eat Out My Heart Anymore" are especially entrancing Michael Jackson performances.

In 1980, Motown released twenty albums which they called their "Motown Superstar Series," featuring all re-released material. Much of the material was presented in a new way: medleys comprised of five or six of each artist's hits mixed together end-to-end with the bass and drums augmented with new tracks to make them "disco-ized." This was successful with some of the medley's, for instance in the case of *Diana Ross & The Supremes*. However, the medley that was made for "The Jackson Five/Motown Superstar Series Volume 12" album, is an artistically unsuccessful mess combining fast songs with ballads. The second side contains five un-touched repackaged hits. The release "Michael Jackson/Motown Superstar Series Volume 7" is simply a re-release of two sides of Michael's Motown hit recordings.

Also in 1980, another member of the Jackson family released a first solo album: LaToya Jackson. Her debut disc, entitled "LaToya Jackson" is on the Polydor label, and featured two chart hits, "Night Time Lover" and "If You Feel The Funk." Although the later tune made it to number forty on the charts, the former cut peaked at Number Fifty-nine and is the better song. That same song, "Night Time Lover" was written by LaToya and Michael, and was produced and arranged by Michael.

In 1981, Polydor released LaToya's second album, "My Special Love." The hit exotic dance number "Stay The Night" received the most attention (as a single it reached Number Thirty-one). I feel that the song "Camp Kuchi Kaiai" was less predictable, and more fun in feeling. When I interviewed LaToya in New York City in July of that year, I commented how I liked that "Camp" song with the funny title. LaToya laughed, and explained, " 'Camp Kuchi Kaiai!' . . . it's a camp that takes place in the movie that Katharine Hepburn did with Henry Fonda."

"You mean 'On Golden Pond,' " I said of the film which had yet to be released. "Did you go to that camp?" I asked.

"Actually," she continued, "Michael went to the camp. Michael went on the set for a month; he and Jane together, and they stayed in a cabin, and watched Katharine and Henry shoot . . . the entire month. So, he came back from the camp with all these tee-shirts, 'Camp Kuchi Kaiai.' I asked him, 'What is it?' and he said it's a little thing that takes place in the movie, Camp Kuchi Kaiai, and so I used the title in the song!"

1981 saw the appearance of the Michael Jackson album "One Day In Your Life," which was a compilation of ten of his non-hit single ballads. It really is quite a nice re-package, and the title track, originally debuted on his 1975 album "Forever, Michael." "One Day In Your Life" was released as a single, and made it to number Forty-two on the record charts, but couldn't compete with the singles Michael had out on Epic Records. Five of the album's selections originally appeared on albums by *The Jackson Five*. That brings the total of Michael Jackson solo Motown albums to five original albums, and three repackages. Talk about getting their money's worth out of Michael's recordings!

At this point in time, Michael was becoming quite famous in Hollywood circles, and was acknowledged by the motion picture community's elite "old guard." Michael even met his idol Fred Astaire.

"The first time I met him, I saw in 'TV Guide' that he was on 'The Tonight Show,' so I ran down to the NBC studios in L.A. We started talking, and he said, 'You don't know it, but I already know all about you!' He used to see me on my bike in Beverly Hills!"

Michael also met Jane Fonda. She was at a Hollywood party, and while she was filming "On Golden Pond" with Henry Fonda and Katharine Hepburn in New Hampshire, she invited him along to the set. "When I was on the 'Golden Pond' set," Michael recalls, "I stayed with Jane in the cabin, and we were all alone there on the water and we'd just talk, talk, talk about everything. It was the greatest education for me— she'd learn and I'd learn, and we'd just play off of each other. We talked about all kinds of things, you name it: politics, philosophers, racism, Vietnam, acting, all kinds of things. It was magic."

One of his biggest thrills, was meeting and becoming friends with Katharine Hepburn. "We hit it off great!" he exclaims, "I was kinda scared to meet her at first, because Jane warned me she'll tell you right to your face if she doesn't like you . . . but she did. I feel honored to know her because there are a lot of people she doesn't like. But, right away, she invited me to dinner that day. Ever since then we've been friends.

She came to our concert—the first concert she had ever been to—at the (Madison Square) Garden, and she just enjoyed herself. We call each other on the phone and she sends me letters. She's just wonderful. I went to her house in New York and she showed me Spencer Tracy's favorite chair and his private things in his closet, his little knick-knacks.''

Michael also became friendly with Henry Fonda, and on a couple of occasions had long talks, and/or went fishing. When he died, Michael was one of the people who went over to be with Fonda's widow Shirlee, and his children Jane and Peter. ''The night that Henry Fonda died, I went over there and I was with the family. They were talking and watching all the different news pieces. Although her father died, Jane was still able to show interest in my career, asking me have I gotten the film (''Peter Pan'') yet, and I thought that was very sweet. I think that they had been expecting him to die for so long. Months and months and months ago she was talking as though it was going to be any day. It happened and there were tears sometimes, and laughter sometimes.''

Although it had been four years since *The Jackson Five* left Motown Records, for that entire time there had been lawsuits pending. The March 19, 1980 issue of *Variety* ran the following item:

>   *"Motown Record Corp. has settled its three-year-old, $20,000,000 breach of contract suit against CBS Records and* The Jacksons *group for approximately $600,000, Motown Vice-chairman Michael Roshkind reported.*
>
>   *Jacksons will pay Motown $100,000 under terms*

of the settlement agreement. They have also agreed on other items estimated to be in excess of $500,000. Also as part of the settlement, Motown has retained rights to the name Jackson 5, *the group's handle at the time it was recording for Motown.*

Group ankled the label for a CBS pact in 1975, when Motown originally filed suit. In mid-1976, a Superior Court judge ruled that the group's seven-year Motown pact had expired, freeing them to record for CBS.

Motown, however, continued to press its case, filing an amended cross complaint for damages, the action just now settled. Complaint charged CBS, The Jacksons *and Jackson/Arons Enterprises with breach of contract, interference with prospective advantage, service mark infringement, injurious falsehood, intentional infliction of emotional distress and invasion of privacy."*

In *The New York Daily News* Roshkind was further quoted in reference to "The Jackson Five" title, "We can do anything we want with it. After all, we created the group, created the name. There were 40,000 Jacksons running around, and we not only made five of them stars, we put them in their own house, paid for their education—and worked a full year with them before they cut their first record." Do you get the feeling Motown Records was angry that Michael Jackson and his four brothers left the company?

In 1981, Michael and *The Jacksons* launched a thirty-nine-city concert tour of the United States. The tour commenced in Memphis, Tennessee on July 9, and ended with a record-breaking sold-out four-night stint at

The Los Angeles Forum. On the tour, *The Jacksons* performed for over 600,000 people. The tour had many highlights, including a date at Atlanta's Omni arena as a benefit for The Atlanta Children's Foundation, which was set up to solve the horrible murders that were taking place there at the time. The *Jacksons* raised and donated $100,000 to the fund, and grossed on the whole tour $5.5 million!

During the tour, Michael gave a statement to Robert Hilburn of *The Los Angeles Times*. "This is my last tour," he claimed. "I love being on stage, but I don't like the other things that go with touring. I didn't even want to do this tour. It was going to be canceled except that we wanted to do the benefit for the children in Atlanta.

"I think it's important to grow, and I've been doing this for so long I sometimes feel like I should be seventy by now. We've been around the world twice, performed before kings and ambassadors. It's time to move on. I still want to make records, but I also want to do films. That's how I want to spend my time the next few years."

When *The Jacksons* played at New York City's Madison Square Garden, there were many admiring stars in the audience. Beside Katharine Hepburn, who attended with her niece Katharine Houghton (who starred with her aunt in "Guess Who's Coming To Dinner"), also present to see Michael and his brothers were Andy Warhol, Margot Kidder, Dan Aykroyd, Jane Fonda, Steven Spielberg, Victoria Principal, Andy Gibb, Quincy Jones, Cher, Tatum O'Neal, Lesley Gore, Jamie Lee Curtis and Kristy McNichol.

A great two-record set album entitled "The Jacksons

Live" was recorded and released to capture the event. Released on Epic Records, the album is not only a well-recorded set of fine entertainment by *The Jacksons,* but it is their only "live" album, and commemorates twelve years of record smashes. For Michael it combines on one album all of the phases of his career. From the *Jackson Five* days there is a medley of "I Want You Back/ABC/The Love You Save" plus a great version of "I'll Be There." From his solo Motown days, there's "Ben." From *The Jacksons'* Epic LP's there's "Can You Feel It," "Things I Do For You," "Lovely One," "Shake Your Body (Down To The Ground)," and "Heartbreak Hotel." And, from Michael's "Off The Wall" album came the title cut, "She's Out Of My Life," "Working Day And Night," "Rock With You," and "Don't Stop 'Til You Get Enough." It's very well recorded, and shows off Michael in fine form throughout. "The Jacksons Live" gives an excellent demonstration of the energy and artistry that typifies Michael's phenomenal career. However, for Michael Jackson . . . the best was still yet to come . . .

8

Michael Jackson: "Thriller!"

"Hi, I'm Michael! I used to be little and cute. Now I'm big and cute." he once said from the stage of Radio City Music Hall. But for Michael Jackson, 1982 was the year that he was going to prove that he was not only cute and charming, but that he could create some of the best-selling music in the history of the record industry.

Michael is a very creative person, in many areas of artistic endeavor. "I love to draw—pencil, ink pen—I love art," he confesses. "When I go on tour and visit museums in Holland, Germany or England—you know those huge paintings?—I'm just amazed. You don't think a painter could do something like that. I can look at a piece of sculpture or a painting and totally lose myself in it. Standing there watching it and becoming part of the scene. It can draw tears, it can touch you so much. See, that's where I think the actor or performer should be—to touch that truth inside of the person.

Touch that reality so much that they become a part of what you're doing and you can take them anywhere you want to. You're happy, they're happy. Whatever the human emotion, they're right there with you.

"I love realism." he continues, "I don't like plastics. Deep down inside we're all the same. We all have the same emotions and that's why a film like 'E.T.' touches everybody. Who doesn't want to fly like Peter Pan? Who doesn't want to fly with some magic creature from outer space and be friends with him?"

During 1982, Michael was involved in three different recording projects. He produced and wrote the song "Muscles" for Diana Ross, he sang on and narrated the storybook album "E.T. The Extra-Terrestrial," and recorded his second solo album for Epic Records, "Thriller." Since he had such luck with his collaboration with Quincy Jones on "Off The Wall," Michael chose to team with Jones again for both "Thriller" and "E.T."

One of the first things that was recorded for "Thriller" was the song that teamed him up with the phenomenal Paul McCartney, the duet recording of Michael's composition "The Girl Is Mine." At the same time that was recorded by Michael and Paul, they also created two additional songs, "Say, Say, Say" and "The Man" for McCartney's "Tug Of War" follow-up album. Paul commented before it's release, "The song I've just done with Michael Jackson, you could say it's shallow," said Paul. "There was even a word 'doggone,' that I wouldn't have put in it. When I checked it out with Michael, he explained that he wasn't going for depth—he was going for rhythm, he was going for feel. And he was right. It's not the lyrics that are important on this particular song—it's much more the noise, the performance; my voice, his voice.'' Well the combination was obviously a success, as the song was the first single released from ''Thriller,'' and was ''Number One'' on the Soul and Easy Listening charts, and ''Number Two'' on the pop charts. The only song that blocked it from the Number One spot on the Pop charts was ''Down Under'' by Australian newcomers *Men At Work.* ''The Girl Is Mine'' was the first of five ''Top Ten'' million-selling singles off of ''Thriller.''

Said Michael at the time, ''Paul was just here and we wrote the song 'The Girl Is Mine,' which we sing together on my album. We're fighting over this girl in the song and it came out beautifully. For his album, we wrote and sang two songs together, his 'Tug Of War Part II.' But for mine it's the song that I wrote. There's a rap at the end where we're fighting over her. It's funny. I was coming back from England working on Paul McCartney's album, zooming along on the Concorde, and this song popped into my head. I said, 'Hey, that's perfect for Diana!' I didn't have a tape recorder or anything, so I had to suffer for like three hours. Soon as I got home I whipped that baby on tape.''

The song was ''Muscles,'' and it became a ''Top Ten'' smash for Diana, and went on to be nominated for a Grammy Award.

From the minute it opened in June of 1982, ''E.T. The Extra-Terrestrial'' (the movie) was an instant box-office hit. It charmed young and old viewers alike, and quickly became one of the all-time box-office record-setters. A cross between a sentimental ''Lassie'' movie, and a science fiction film about creatures from space, ''E.T.'' had the entire country sitting in darkened theaters and crying for the plight of the "weird squashy little guy with a head shaped like an eggplant!" It was truly the "space age" rendition of "clapping to keep Tinkerbell alive."

The film was such a smash that suddenly there were "E.T." lunchboxes, "E.T." games, "E.T." tee-shirts, "E.T." notebooks, "E.T." picture books, "E.T." coloring books, "E.T." dolls, etc. etc. etc. Despite the over-merchandising of the little man from space, who looked like a "Naugahyde" chair with eyes the size of golfballs, the story was genuinely touching and everyone could identify with it. Amongst the film's biggest fans is Michael Jackson. Speaking of director Steven Spielberg's artistry with the movie, Michael analyzed, "Steven went straight to the heart. He knows—when in doubt, go for the heart."

There was already an ethereal-sounding soundtrack album by Academy Award winning composer John Williams, but how about a storybook album narrated by someone with universal appeal, and a sense of genuine youthful wonderment; someone with a lot of appeal and heartfelt emotionalism . . . someone like Michael Jackson. Suddenly Steven Spielberg, Quincy Jones and Michael had the same vision. At the time Michael explained, "It's a storybook album, and I'm narrating the whole story and singing a song. We've been just meeting and talking about making it the all-time storybook album." And that's just what they did.

"That album is a little new for me, because I've never narrated a story," continued Michael, but he mastered another arena of artistry, and did a great job.

With a narrative written by William Kotzwinkle, Steven Spielberg, Quincy Jones, and Peggy Lipton Jones

(Quincy's wife, and former star of TV's "Mod Squad").
The song that Michael sang is one of the most beautiful
ballads that he has ever performed. It is entitled
"Someone In The Dark" with music by Rod Temperton,
and lyrics by Alan and Marilyn Bergman (they wrote
amongst other tunes "The Way We Were"). The
combination, sewn together with Quincy's production,
dialogue from the film, and Michael's effective and
emotional reading of the narrative with grand soaring
orchestrations by John Williams is such an masterful
production that "E.T. The Extra-Terrestrial" illicits as
many tears as the movie does.

The record, and the special cassette version, both
come as deluxe boxed sets, with a complete script-style
full color story book of dialogue and narration, and
best of all, a great full-color poster of Michael Jackson
and E.T.! MCA Records had obtained a release for
Michael's services on the recording, and knew that the
album, and Michael's song had a lot of potential. They
therefore planned a lot of promotion, and even pressed
a single version of Michael's "Someone In The Dark,"
which was sent out to radio stations. However, at the
same time, CBS was getting ready to ship "Thriller"
to the stores for Christmas, and that's where the trouble
began.

In the November 27, 1982 edition of *Billboard*
magazine, the LP headed the page of that weeks "Top
Album Picks," and questioned in the first line of the
review, "How long can the 'E.T.' boom last?" The
trouble was outlined on the front page of that same
issue:

"NEW YORK—CBS Records wants to send 'E.T.' home to the warehouses of MCA Records, and has taken that label to court to achieve its objective.

In an action filed Nov. 10 in New York Supreme Court, CBS is seeking to block sales of MCA's $11.98 storybook album of 'E.T. The Extra-Terrestrial,' featuring narration and vocal performance by Michael Jackson, an Epic artist.

CBS claims that MCA interfered with its contractual relationship with Jackson, noting that while the artist was allowed to record a song ('Someone In The Dark') for inclusion in the 'E.T.' storybook, this was on condition that the package not be marketed before Christmas, and that Jackson's performance not be released as a single.

After being turned down for a temporary restraining order, CBS is seeking a preliminary injunction against MCA.

The CBS suit claims: 'The acts of MCA in obtaining master recordings of Jackson's performance, in distributing to radio stations a single version of that performance, in advertising and preparing to release, distribute and sell to the public phonograph records containing and featuring Jackson and bearing his name, and in releasing its album, 'The E.T. Storybook,' prior to CBS' release of (Jackson's) album 'Thriller,' were and are being done willfully, and with the intent, purpose and design of unfairly competing with CBS.' "

To make a long story short, CBS "killed" the single version of "Someone In The Dark," and "The E.T. Storybook" never posed any threat to the success of what was about to come, "Thriller." From this transaction comes the ultimate Michael Jackson collector's item . . . the 45 version of "Someone In The Dark" that was serviced to radio stations only.

According to Bob Dudnick, lawyer for MCA, "If CBS has a case against us, then we have a case against Michael Jackson. Michael Jackson's representatives knew all along we planned to release the record before Christmas." Just like Elliott struggled to retain custody of E.T., CBS and MCA fought for the rights to "The E.T. Storybook" record.

The next of Michael's recordings to be released was the mega-album to end them all, the ultimate "Thriller." When it was released in December of 1982, it immediately won critical acclaim. It entered "Billboard" magazine's album charts the week of December 25, as the Number Eleven LP in the country. The next week it became the Number Nine album, and had yet to leave the "Top Ten" by the Fall of 1983.

The critical acclaim for "Thriller" was unanimous:

—". . . irresistible pulse and energy . . ."
Billboard

—"Willingness to experiment and a flawless sense of rhythm make this an album that lives up to its title."

People

—"Jackson reworks familiar romantic themes with his sky-walking falsetto and deliciously stylish delivery, in a slick, rapid-fire production reminiscent of his past hits."
Variety

105

—"'Thriller' is a sleek and sharp machine, a work of amazing confidence and pacing . . ."
High Fidelity

—"Michael Jackson's flamboyant 'Thriller' lives up to its title . . . super-spectacular production . . . gripping performances . . . a thunderstorm of rhythmic and vocal effects."
Stereo Review

—". . . sheer vitality . . . another watershed in the creative development of this prodigiously talented performer . . . spunky . . . fiery conviction . . . gorgeous . . ."
Rolling Stone

—". . . superbly crafted . . . with a pervasive confidence infusing the album as a whole, 'Thriller' suggests that Mr. Jackson's evolution as an artist is far from finished. He is, after all, only 24 years old."
New York Times

Michael Jackson began the year 1983 riding the crest of the most successful album in his career and the most successful solo album ever recorded by a male vocalist in the history of recorded music.

The week of January 22, 1983 the second single from "Thriller" was released: "Billie Jean." After three weeks on the charts it became the Number One song in the country, tying a record set three times in 1970 by *The Jackson Five:* "ABC," "The Love You Save," and "I'll Be There." Each hit the Number One spot three weeks after their release.

The week of March 5, 1983 "Beat It" was released as a single, and the following week Michael Jackson became the first Black artist to simultaneously have the Number One album and single in the United States and Great Britain.

At this point in time a successful new media phenomenon had taken the music industry by storm and called itself "M-TV." The syndicated cable T.V. show revolutionized record promotion and became a state-of-the-art medium unto itself. M-TV's programming is comprised of record company-produced "mini-musical" versions of hit songs starring the artists that made the hits. One of the major criticisms of M-TV was that its "rock" format was racist. Black artists including an especially verbal Rick James had yet to crack the M-TV play list. The only Black artist at that time to break into M-TV was Tina Turner and her concert footage of "Ball Of Confusion," but that was only on a "light rotation" basis. In March of 1983 "Billie Jean" got her M-TV! Michael's ambitious version of the hot song was the most exciting video that had been produced to date. It was topped the next month by Bob Giraldi's direction of the "Beat It" video. Resembling a steamy sequence from "West Side Story," Michael's "Beat It" video cost Epic Records an estimated $100,000.00.

The week of April 9, 1983, in its sixth week as Number One, "Billie Jean" became Michael's best selling single both solo and with *The Jackson Five*. His other number one pop hit singles were: "I'll Be There," "Rock With You," "ABC," "The Love You Save," "I Want You Back," "Ben," and "Don't Stop 'Til You

Get Enough." "Beat It" joined that list in April of 1983. Michael's next two singles from "Thriller," "Wanna Be Startin' Somethin' " and "Human Nature" became the record-breaking fourth and fifth "Top Ten" singles respectively.

Michael's composition on the album included: "Beat It," "Billie Jean," "Wanna Be Startin' Somethin'," and "The Girl Is Mine." Steve Porcaro (of "Toto") and John Bettis wrote "Human Nature," James Ingram ("Baby Come To Me") and Quincy Jones composed "P.Y.T. (Pretty Young Thing)," and Rod Temperton penned "The Lady In My Life," "Baby Be Mine," and "Thriller." Special guest appearances on the album included Eddie Van Halen's searing guitar solo on "Beat It," Janet and LaToya Jackson's background vocals on "P.Y.T.," and Vincent Price's wicked rap on the song "Thriller."

On Monday, May 16, 1983 NBC-TV broadcast the two hour prime-time special "Motown 25: Yesterday, Today, Forever." On the show Smokey Robinson reunited with *The Miracles*, Diana re-joined *The Supremes*, and the original *Jackson Five* performed for the first time since 1976. Michael however, "stole the show" with his rendition of "Billie Jean." The show went on to become the highest rated broadcast of that week and went on to win several Emmy Award Nominations.

Michael himself was nominated for an Emmy in the category "Best Individual Performance On A Variety Or Music Program." When the awards were handed out on "live" television September 25, 1983, Michael's "Billie Jean" performance again stirred excitement when the clip was shown, unfortunately he did not receive the Emmy statuette, Leontyne Price won it for her appearance on the PBS broadcast "Live From Lincoln Center." However, the special, "Motown 25: Yesterday, Today, Forever" received a top award as "Best Variety Music Or Comedy Program."

The show was such a success that it was re-broadcast on October 30, 1983. To capitalize upon the show's popularity Motown released a series of re-packaged albums by the artists who appeared on the show. This included the seventeenth *Jackson Five* album to be released by Motown, "Great Songs And Performances That Inspired The Motown 25th Anniversary T.V. Special by Michael Jackson and The Jackson 5. (How's that for a long album title?)

Not only did "Thriller" revolutionize Michael's career but it was also credited with pulling CBS Records firmly "into the black." *Cash Box* magazine dubbed Michael "the savior of the record business," and *The Los Angeles Harold Examiner* music critic Mikal Gilmore reported "Just as Elvis Presley and *The Beatles* helped galvanize stagnating industries in their eras, so can Jackson . . . help unify an audience large and diverse enough to count as a genuine mass consensus." *The Los Angeles Times* in its July 24, 1983 issue reported that "CBS has rebounded in 1983. The first-quarter profit increase of 101% was the best January-to-March performance in the unit's history. The gain was sparked by such artists as Michael Jackson whose 'Thriller' album has produced four hit singles and sold more than eight million copies—best since the industry's glory days of 1978."

Success usually sparks greed and such was the case in June of 1983 when "Billboard" magazine revealed that Michael's managers were fighting for control of his career. At the time that "Thriller" was released, Michael had dual management, utilizing both the services of Wiesner/DeMann Entertainment, and of his father Joe Jackson. In March both of his contracts had lapsed and Michael renewed neither of them. It was then that the bickering began. The June 25, 1983 issue of *Billboard* turned up the following information:

"With regard to Wiesner/DeMann Entertainment Joe Jackson was quoted as saying, 'They have been put on notice and it (their contract) will not be renewed. As far as I'm concerned it's over. They don't have a contract and my boys are not resigning with them. There are a lot of leeches trying to break up the group (The Jacksons). A lot of people are whispering in Michael's ear but they know who they are. They're only in it for the money. I was there before it started and I'll be there after it ends.' "

According to Joe Jackson, Wiesner/DeMann were brought into the picture, "because there was a time when I felt I needed White help in dealing with the corporate structure at CBS, and thought they'd be able to help. But they never gave me the respect you expect from a business partner."

Apprised of his father's statement, in that same issue of *Billboard*, Michael resounded, "I don't know what would make him say something like that. To hear him talk like that turns my stomach. I don't know where he gets that from. I happen to be color-blind. I don't hire color; I hire competence. The individual can be of any race or creed as long as I get the best. I am president of my organization, and I have the final word on every decision. Racism is not my motto. One day I strongly expect every color to live as one family."

According to Ron Wiesner in the exact same issue of *Billboard*, "That's Joe's personal point of view. There's no great love between us, and it's no big secret. I haven't talked to the man in six months. But we have no problem with Michael or *The Jacksons*. The problem seems to be with their father more than with anybody. We're the only ones who deal with the record company. Joe, doesn't talk to anybody up there. He doesn't have any relationship, and from what I gather, he doesn't want to."

At the same time Freddy DeMann said, "Joe made the deal with us, but since then we've worked directly with the group—with Michael and *The Jacksons*. He hasn't been involved in any of the major issues for the past five years. We don't have a good relationship with him, but I don't think he enjoys a good relationship with anyone whose skin is not Black. We're in the process of putting together several deals on Michael's behalf and at his request. He has specifically instructed us to pursue record and film opportunities for him, and we will be involved in the next Jackson's album and *The Jacksons'* tour (set for spring 1983).

As of the Fall of 1983 this problem had not yet been resolved. In early October, I personally attempted to contact Ron Weisner for further comment, but he refused to supply any further information. With regard to the Michael Jackson issue, the answer was strictly "No comment."

Since Michael had begun to experience this explosive new success, the only major press interview he granted was for the cover of "Rolling Stone," in their February

17, 1983 edition. According to Epic Records' publicity director Eliot Hubbard, "I've been turning down offers left and right, from *Vogue*, *Glamour*, you name it." Michael wasn't talking to anyone.

Late in the summer of 1983 Michael went into a recording studio to perform a revolutionary duet with Barbra Streisand. Also released, was a new version of "Thriller" . . . the "Picture Disc" which features photos of Michael pressd in-between layers of clear vinyl and playable on any stereo.

On September 27, the sixth single from the "Thriller" album, "P.Y.T. (Pretty Young Thing)" was released. Also at the end of September it was announced that by surpassing the sales figure of fourteen million copies worldwide, "Thriller" had become the largest-selling album in the history of CBS Records. The singles alone at that time had exceeded twelve million copies worldwide (five million in the United States alone).

"Thriller" had racked up thirty-seven awards for Michael from around the globe, and hit the Number One spot on charts in eight countries outside the United States. The following is the official CBS tally as of September 1983:

—Canada (Quintuple Platinum)
—United Kingdom (Triple Platinum)
—Holland (Triple Platinum)
—Australia (Triple Platinum)
—New Zealand (Triple Platinum)
—Japan (Platinum)
—Germany (Platinum)
—France (Platinum)
—Sweden (Platinum)

—Belgium (Platinum)
—Switzerland (Platinum)
—Spain (Platinum)
—Greece (Platinum)
—South Africa (Platinum)
—Denmark (Gold)
—Italy (Gold)
—Israel (Gold)
—Norway (Silver)

On top of that, "Billie Jean" went Number One in eight countries outside the United States, and "Beat It" went Number One in six countries outside the United States.

Michael finished the year 1983 virtually at the top of the entertainment world!

9

Michael Jackson—Video Star

Not only will 1983 be remembered for "Thriller," but it will also be revered as the year that M-TV took over America. Suddenly across the United States, you could not only listen to your favorite artists in your own home, but you could also enjoy them acting out their musical fantasies in stereophonic living color on video twenty-four hours a day!

Michael Jackson's video presentations were two of the most significant works to be captured on videotape, and are already considered "classics" in their own right. On both "Billie Jean" and "Beat It" Michael demonstrated more confidence, flair and energy than were ever shown in his performance in "The Wiz." Both were filmed as capsulated movie epics, each possessing all of the right elements to make them into virtual video/visual short stories. The short scenerios set new standards in video creativity and spread Michael's popularity to new heights, especially the one for "Beat It."

The opening to the "Billie Jean" video shows a trench-coated spy snuffing out the butt-end of his cigarette onto the pavement of a grimy city alleyway. Cut to a shiny silver dollar coin being flipped into the hazy evening air. The picture turns from black & white to color as it focuses in on a two-toned pair of shoes stepping into view. Cut to the silver dollar still flipping in and out of the hand. Cut to Michael Jackson watching his hand flip the coin. While all of this is going on, his actions are being viewed and noted by the trench-coated spy hiding in the damp darkness.

As we peer deeper into the alleyway, we run into a drunken bum, passed out against a wall, with his head resting on a garbage can, his filthy coffee cup lies in the foreground awaiting coins. Michael looks down on the bum and flips his silver coin into the bum's cup. The cup instantly glows with a mysterious inner-light, and suddenly the begger's rags disappear into the white light, and "presto chango" he is wearing a white tux with a red cummerbund and a red silk bowtie! For all of this activity Michael's hit song "Billie Jean" is serving as the narrative soundtrack.

Out of the alley, the street is deserted, as the spy runs for cover amid the strewn newspapers and trash that is blowing in the wind. Michael, in his black leather pants, strawberry-ice-cream pink shirt, red bowtie, and iridescent white socks, pops out of the alley. As he walks along the sidewalk, each square of the sidewalk that his feet touch, glows from beneath. Putting his foot up onto a trash can, he draws a leopard hankerchief out of his back pocket, and begins to wipe clean the white side of the black and white shoe. As he turns away the hankerchief is suddenly a leopard cub that darts across the street.

As the sound of ''Billie Jean'' continues unfolding, Michael meanders down the sidewalk past the window displays of small shops and stores, looking very dejected and blue. He walks past a men's clothing store, and a camera shop. When he reaches a lamppost that he decides to lean upon, it glows white from within, at his mere touch. The spy, in the meantime, sneaks up from behind Michael, and just as he's about to put a gag around his mouth, a Polaroid SX-70 Autofocus 660 model instant camera goes off in the window. As the ejected piece of Polaroid film develops, we see the image of the spy, but no Michael. He has vanished.

Cut to Michael on the road out of town, his jacket slung over his right shoulder ala Frank Sinatra as he verbally denies the paternity suit described in the song: ''Billie Jean's not my girl!'' he violently protests. In a series of split frame shots, pans, zooms, and freeze-frame shots; Michael goes into his dance, spinning, pirouetting, and going up on the points of his toes midstep! He points his fingers accusingly at the air, and does double spins in lightning-fast time and whips his arms into the sleeves of the jacket, and pulls the quilted leather collar up around him. His only dance partners are two girls on a billboard, and a desolate city scape.

Cut to a bedroom with a white canopy-covered bed, then . . . to the spy in the trench coat, and then again to Michael still singing on the winding road out of town.

Back in the alley, Michael creeps up a flight of stairs to view the bed. There is the form of someone in the bed, under the white sheets. Still under the surveillance

117

of the spy, Michael throws back the sheet and climbs into the bed, and as he does, it glows with white heat like everything else he has touched. As the police arrive, Michael mysteriously disappears in the bed, again vanishing into thin air.

In the final scene of "Billie Jean," as the police lead the handcuffed spy away, the camera cuts to the sidewalk, where the leopard hankerchief, and a progression of lit sidewalk tiles mark Michael's footsteps, off into the distance and away from the camera. *Finis*.

Without a doubt the hottest and most talked about video presentation of the entire year was Michael Jackson's "Beat It." Directed with cinematic flair by award-winning Bob Giraldi, the video contained superb camera work, choreography by Michael Peters, and visual styling by Jill Klein.

The video has been compared to a mini-version of "West Side Story," with its 1980's updated version of warring street gangs, pent-up inner-city aggressions, and a melodramatic look at the macho ethic of being "cool." It has been publicly spoken of as an epic milestone in music videos, and with due reason. It is a masterpiece that virtually had home video tape players "working day and night" to make it the most recorded music video of the Summer of 1983!

The scenerio of the opening footage of "Beat It" begins moments before the familiar thumping beats of the song's intro. It finds us in a greasy diner following the steps of two mean dudes in hats and leather, on their way out into the hot summer Los Angeles night. As the duo leave the diner through the swinging doors, the right-hand door swings back toward the screen, and the first beat of the song begins.

Outside, six colorfully dressed gang members appear sequentially and then turn, jump, and run toward the night's menu of street trouble. People suddenly crawl out of every pore of the city to see the fight that is to ensue, from manholes below, and from pool halls above. There's a rumble in the wind, and it's clear that no one wants to miss out on the latest confrontation of gangland warfare. As the gang leader dressed in white struts toward the designated battlefield of action, Michael's opening lines begin.

Cut to Michael on his bed, in a dimly lit bedroom, clutching his pillow in frustration; should he hit the streets tonight, or avoid the danger and lose face with the gang? The streets below swarm with macho guys heading for the rumble. Michael rolls over on his back on the bed, revealing his tee shirt with piano keys on the front. He springs from the bed and rationalizes "It doesn't matter who's wrong or right."

On the street they're arriving by the truckload. As Michael steps out of the front door of his apartment, dressed in a red leather jacket and with fire in his eyes, he delivers his approach to violence in the hallway: "Beat it!" (as in "turn the other cheek and walk away!") It seems that Michael has made up his mind to give the young punks a piece of his mind before they rumble.

The longshots of the gangs in the alleys, approaching the designated warehouse, are magnificent. Steam rises from the streetbed as opposing armies march towards the arena.

Michael bursts through the swinging doors of the greasy diner . . . no one's there. He reels over to the counter of the diner's fountain area, and spins a few of the swiveling counter chairs in anger and passion. He

119

slides into the pool hall . . . no one's there either. As he sings his message, Michael pivots, gavots, points and turns with the grace of a trained dancer, and the conviction of a leader. "Beat it!" he exclaims as his motions punctuate the night air.

Meanwhile, at the warehouse, garage doors rise, and the gangs are all there! As we survey the crowd that has assembled, it's a potpourri of thugs, each one meaner than the next. It's the leader in white, and the leader in black, ready to duel. They swagger towards each other and extend opposite arms, and are promptly tied to each other at the wrist with rope. The switchblades whip out, and they prepare to do the "dance of death" with blades flailing. They spin, swoop and lunge towards each other's chests with the gleaming knives.

Snapping his fingers and bouncing to the beat, Michael jumps into action as he descends into the den of hoods. "It doesn't matter who's wrong or right!" he preaches, and in an instant the whole warehouse is bopping to the beat that Michael has laid down.

They ferociously spin and swirl in a triangular formation, with Michael at it's apex: the "thriller" himself converting the coolest of the cool. The kicks, the leaps, and the spins that make up this syncronized series of precision steps is unmatched in its professionalism, and its sheer electricity. Often bordering on break dancing, the scene is movie magic in its essence. As the cameras draw back at the end of the song, you feel that your breath has just been taken away.

In the October 1983 issue of *Record* magazine, director Bob Giraldi reported to writer Alan Hecht, how "Beat It" came about. "I had listened to his record and wanted to do the 'Billie Jean' video, but his managers had already lined up a British director for it. After that they decided that 'Beat It' would be done by somebody else. So, I was in Santo Domingo with my family, Antony (Payne, his producer) was in New York, Michael was in California, and we kept trying to call each other. Did you ever try to call anybody in Santo Domingo? One day my wife picked up the phone and she hears, 'Hello, is Bob there?' It was Michael Jackson. Anyway we talked, and he told me it was a go. He said the song to him was nothing more than turning the other cheek. Michael Jackson's never been in a gang war; Michael Jackson's probably never been out of that house! I think the world knows he's been watched and protected all his life. He just said, 'Let's do something street.' ''

Said Bob of the actual Los Angeles street gang members who were used in the film along with the professional dancers, ''They were brought to us by a combination of The Los Angeles Police Department, my production company and Ron Weisner. The police warned us to be very careful. We were, and I've never had a more wonderful experience in my life as a director than watching these tough gangs. They were taking my direction, but they were skeptical, dubious. Watching the dance sequence start to happen, they looked at each other as if to say, 'Now there's some of our brothers doing something that none of us will ever be able to do.' And they found another kind of macho from the piece. From that point on we were home free. I think violence stinks. The whole beauty of 'Beat It' is how it shows that the macho trip is a joke. I had peace come through in this magical creature named Michael Jackson. Obviously, if anybody ever analyzes it properly they will see that it's anti-violence, not pro-violence.''

In September of 1983, Giraldi spoke candidly to Fred Goodman of *Cash Box* magazine about the videos that he was becoming famous for: Diana Ross' "Pieces Of Ice," Pat Benetar's "Love Is A Battlefield," and of course Michael Jackson's "Beat It." These are some of the comments that Giraldi made while he was preparing to do the video presentation of Michael Jackson and Paul McCartney's "Say, Say, Say."

"Money," laughed Giraldi of his reasoning for going from television commercials into music video. "Money and the chance to fall in love with my idols. No, it certainly wasn't money because I don't make anywhere near as much doing music videos as I do making television commercials. And it certainly wasn't for lack of work. It was, as we say around here, because it was the very next thing. Everything around here revolves around us not doing projects that are like the ones we do six weeks before. Initially, we didn't talk about about me doing them, because in fact they don't offer a very big profit margin. But when the first one, 'lo and behold,' became Michael Jackson, I realized, 'Well, I'm not gonna give that to anyone else.' I loved the song. 'Thriller' was hot but of course it wasn't the album that it is now, and I said 'Let's go for it!'

"It's been said in a few articles inadvertently that I would use this medium as a stepping stone to feature films. That is totally untrue. I don't do it because my eye is on feature films; I do it because my eye is on Michael Jackson's 'Beat It,' and I don't love Hollywood!"

"Michael Jackson has obvious talent!" claims Giraldi. "Pat Benetar's risk was far greater, and I have a warm spot in my heart for her because she went to that studio and did not get intimidated. She worked with Michael Peters, our choreographer, and she worked and worked and worked until she could do something which I think looks quite good. But she laid it all out there. Diana Ross was a little bit more protective of herself. She did what she can do because she's a fashionable lady and feels the most comfortable when she's looking the most beautiful. Michael is magnificent as a dancer and a performer. His acting came through his performing. Pat had to dance—something she couldn't do—and she had to act—something she really hadn't done professionally before. And I think she's a wonderful actress. If I must say so, I think she has a bigger career than the others in the future as an actress.''

Bob is now concerned with the accusations that he had also pioneered high costs in videos. ''Beat It'' exceeded $100,000 in shooting and post-production. Said Giraldi, ''In an interview a couple of weeks ago in *Los Angeles Magazine*, I was accused by a couple of my peer directors of having enough money to walk into this medium and play and experiment and ruin it for the rest of them. That's crap! I take my work seriously, and I charge accordingly. I charge enough money plus a profit for me to create, conceive, direct and execute my videos properly. You come on to my set and ask Paul McCartney or Michael Jackson or Pat Benatar, and they will tell you that I'm a very professional director. Does that mean that the other guy is doing it unprofessionally? Maybe it does. You know something? My work is better.

''What before was 'put-a-camera-on-my-shoulder-and-experiment' is now a professional medium being overrun by a different kind of professional and I am one of those professionals. I make my kind of film, and I'll put my film and my profit and my integrity against any of them.

"David Bowie, in the same issue of the magazine, said that he hopes that now there won't be a whole lot of 'West Side Story'-type videos. You know what? I wish David Bowie's videos were anywhere near as good as his tracks. His tracks are magnificent, he's a wonderful artist. His videos are amateurish, in my opinion. I don't have to defend myself. I know they're afraid, the young directors who really can't deliver the same kind of movie-making attitude, choreography, sex, attitude and emotion that I can."

Explained Bob, "I do not specifically design any videos to sell records. I design story lines based on my visions and inspirations of what that music means to me. 'Beat It' went back to my childhood, it was the super-macho bull I saw growing up in Patterson, New Jersey. It had nothing whatsoever to do with 'West Side Story.' And Michael Jackson dug it—he said 'Okay, this is my anti-violence statement through music, this is your anti-macho vision as a director. Peace through dance!' "

Did "Beat It" and his other video projects change his outlook on his commercial filming? "Yes," admits Giraldi, "I just did a NARM commercial and I tried to get 'Jellybean' Benitez to mix it. It didn't work, but I inspired them to go out and get a good mixer and do some hot stuff. When I do a McDonald's commercial, McDonald's has to go out and get the best music people, or else it's 'See you later, honey.' Music has changed everything. Look at 'Flashdance.' The story is so shallow that if you dove into it, you'd crack your skull open. But the music keeps me going. We're in a time of music, and music is the concept.''

Says Bob of his approach: ''Try and be different. On one hand David (Bowie) accuses me of doing dance and 'West Side Story,' and I guess he was saying that he likes the experimentation phase better. On the other hand, I think the experimentation phase is absolutely wonderful. But its problem is that it results in a lot of sameness. If anything is sure in any creative medium, it's when you get a winner: 'Jump on it!' You don't think Stevie Nicks' video (''Stand Back'') isn't inspired by 'Beat It?' I know it is. The only problem there is, is that she can't dance.''

Since M-TV has such specific programming policies, Michael's ''Beat It'' made the playlist, but Diana Ross' ''Pieces Of Ice'' did not. How does Giraldi feel about that? ''I want to do Black videos because I enjoy Black music,'' he explains. ''I have no color lines—I'm the most ruthless person in the world and will do what I am inspired and excited by. In retrospect, M-TV probably didn't play 'Pieces Of Ice' because the track wasn't very good. However, you cannot tell me that 'Pieces Of Ice' wasn't as good as 60% of the stuff they play on the air. So why wouldn't they play it? Because saying it wasn't good enough is an excuse for M-TV to do what rock radio stations do. I call it 'racist,' and that may be that they don't agree with crossover and they'll only play Michael Jackson because you have to play Michael since his stuff is the most popular in the world. And Donna (Summer) for whatever reason they play Donna. And Rick James they'll keep off. Now, I think they get off on it, they capitalize on the press on it. I think they love that controversy; it's what sets them apart. I think it's silly.''

At that time, Giraldi was planning to go into production with the video version of Michael Jackson and Paul McCartney's "Say, Say, Say." Previewing his plans, he revealed, "We're gonna try a humorous approach. I think M-TV sorely needs humor. It's a period piece, but it's not a period piece. This one isn't gut level for me—it's out of the music. So I'm not emotionally involved with this one; I'm involved because Paul McCartney is an idol of mine. I think pop videos need some humor. They're too serious and too violent. All that anger and hostitlity that is rock 'n roll can also be boredom. So we're gonna try and do something different."

What Bob Giraldi has managed to do through his work with "Beat It" and "Say, Say, Say" is to successfully show off Michael Jackson's talents in front of the camera in a way that none of his other TV or movie roles have been able to do. "Beat It" drew so much attention that Michael's worth as a movie musical star has quadrupled. His role of the befuddled Scarecrow in "The Wiz" may have put him nicely on the silver screen, but it was "Beat It" that unleashed his charismatic style and sensual movements with confidence, professionalism and flash. It has created a whole new dimension of creativity for Michael Jackson.

10

The Girl Who Gave Him "The Look"

There are thousands of pieces of research to put together in completing a book such as this. One Saturday in September as I was working on this manuscript, while my friend Jack Cunningham was proofreading it, two other friends, David Salidor and Suzan Kressel stopped over for coffee, and to drop off some more material on Michael that I needed.

As we sat drinking coffee, Suzan, who is a buyer for Bloomingdales, mentioned that she had worked on a promotional display that involved a talented twenty-four-year-old designer who lives in California, named Jill Klien. Suzan proceeded to tell me that Jill had worked with Michael as a stylist, picking out clothes for him for the "Billie Jean" video. She suggested that I talk to Jill to get some additional insight into Michael's talent, and his "look."

I called Jill and found that she had quite a few fascinating stories and observations about Michael. She was very helpful in gaining a closer look at Michael, and the distinctive "look" that he has adopted in the past couple of years. Our coast-to-coast telephone conversation went like this:

MARK: What is the difference between Michael's everyday "look" and the one that everyone is going crazy over in his photographs and video presentations?

JILL: Michael is very interesting visually, because when he walks into a room he doesn't exert all that energy that he has on stage. In his everyday life he underdresses himself. He purposely underdresses himself so as to not draw attention to himself, so when you dress him up in the clothes and you put him in front of the camera, there's magic he releases that just blows everyone away! When you've been working on him for the past hour, on hair and makeup and clothes, and when the package is put together it blows you away that this is the same person who walked in the door.

He has a real flair for turning on the magic in front of the camera. And I think that the make-up, and the hair, and the clothes and everything gets him really going. He gets really excited by all that.

MARK: I had read a couple of quotes where he said that he really likes getting into portraying characters. Do you think that he kind of comes to life when he sees what you have come up with for him as a "look?"

JILL: Oh, absolutely. Well, I took an approach that . . . I had heard that Michael liked old movies, and that his favorite star was Fred Astaire. So I took the approach of dressing him in the old 1940's style, "Fred Astaire 'look' " of tying the tie around the waist, the old jackets with the crests on the pockets. You know, the very "princely" put-together look, and Michael flipped over it. And so, he danced as if he was in a Fred Astaire movie . . . you know, the going up on the toes which he took from the old films exactly what he seemed to have cared for, and he loved it.

MARK: Were you the stylist for the latest photo session that he did wearing the yellow sweater with the diamond crest on it? Where did you find that pin?

JILL: Yes . . . where did you find those pictures?

MARK: CBS is using them.

JILL: Oh, I haven't seen them yet. With all of the brothers? We shot all of the brothers together, and some of him by himself.

MARK: I've just seen the ones of him by himself, he's wearing a yellow vest.

JILL: . . . and the bow tie, and he's got diamond pins. I was wearing those, and Michael likes flashy little things and stuff. And, he saw them and he asked if he could wear them, and I said, 'Sure, they'd look great!' And so, there are the four pins put together. We did a cluster of the pins on his sweater.

MARK: So those are four pins that you put together right on the spot there?

JILL: Yes! I had brought some other things that were like military crests and things, but Michael is against anything that even bearly symbolizes war in any way. He was really enchanted by my jewelry and stuff, so we put together the cluster of pins on his vest.

MARK: When was that shooting? CBS dates the photos as circulated in August 1983.

JILL: That shooting was in May.

MARK: And where was that shooting done?

JILL: Matthew Rolston's studio, here in California.

MARK: And Matthew did the shots?

JILL: Yes.

MARK: They're really incredible photos.

JILL: Yes, he's done such beautiful shots of Michael. He did the photos for Andy Warhol's *Interview* magazine, and we shot Michael's poster together. We shot *The Jacksons* together, and we did another publicity shooting with Michael.

130

MARK: Did you pick out Michael's clothes for that shooting?''

JILL: Yes.

MARK: Out of his wardrobe?

JILL: No! Michael usually ends up buying everything that I bring to his shootings, because he loves beautiful clothes, but he has no idea of how to put clothes together personally. He has to have people put them together for him. But no, you would find jeans and plaid shirts in Michael's wardrobe.

MARK: Would you say that you would find him wearing real casual clothes for hanging out?

JILL: For hanging out, Michael doesn't care what he's wearing. But Michael doesn't like to let down the public, as far as his clothes. And he has a real style about . . . he knows good clothes. He knows good things when he sees them, and he's willing to try anything, he's very open-minded.

MARK: So he really has an eye for quality is what you're saying?

JILL: Yes, definitely.

MARK: Where did those clothes from the photo shooting come from, can you say?

JILL: I bought a lot at Maxwell Blues, and at Madonna Man, and Jerry Magnan. And a lot of things I put together. There are shots, I don't know if you've seen them, where I bought a red cardigan sweater, and a "J" crest. This was a big red "J" crest, and he later called me back and ordered one in every color I could find! When he finds something that he likes he wants one of every color that I can get him. He likes very "princely" elegant looking stuff. He won't wear leather; he doesn't like wearing leather because he's a vegetarian.

MARK: He's really against killing animals just for show?

JILL: No, he's really against it. In fact, he's wearing a leather outfit in "Billie Jean" and he's wearing a leather coat in his poster, but you wouldn't catch him wearing that in his everyday dress, it's purely for show. He doesn't like the idea of leather clothes, or of killing animals.

MARK: That leather suit that he wears in the "Billie Jean" video is amazing. Is that a designer piece?

JILL: Yes, I believe that it was designed by his sister-in-law.

MARK: How did you get involved in the "Billie Jean" video.

JILL: Well, I was working with Michael at the time, so I was called to put together shoes, and called to bring this to the studio . . . and what actually got pulled together was from different things. There were many different ideas of what they were going to do.

MARK: So you just arrived at the video shooting with a variety of clothes and accessories?

JILL: Well, before the actual taping, they were planning it months in advance. They ended up going with the black leather tuxedo with the long shawl collar. It was a real good choice for Michael. You know, he is in total control of everything that goes on, which some people may not understand, but he is probably, the most amazing young genius of all the people that I have ever worked with! Because, he has a "say" in every last thing, down to the socks that he puts on. He practically will tell you exactly what he wants, although he wouldn't be able to go out and pick it out himself, or design it. But he has a real flair, and his hands in everything that goes on.

MARK: What you're saying is that he has a general concept, and you just fill in the details.

JILL: Yes, and no one controls him. No one.

MARK: So you find yourself in a basic situation where he defines a "look" that he wants to come up with, and it's up to you to find the clothes that carry that across?

JILL: Yes, or he'll say, "I don't want anything that's going to make me look 'cheap' or 'trendy.'" That's more like the direction he'll give you. He wants to look fine and classy. That's the only direction that I've ever gotten from Michael. From then on, he loved everything that I would bring, but as far as his music goes and the people around him, and what music is played on the stereo while he's shooting, it's all up to Michael.

MARK: Were you on the set for the shooting of the video of "Billie Jean?"

JILL: Yes.

MARK: What was that experience like, and how long did it take to come up with that final presentation?

JILL: I had a feeling that he had that all planned ahead of time. I was only there one day. I was there the first day and then I left. From what I understand from people who worked on it longer, it was the most smoothly run, well organized, put together video that anyone had ever worked on. I have lots of friends who worked with the grips, and stuff like that. They couldn't believe how smoothly it went, because, a lot of times you'll go to a video shooting, and they don't even know what you're going to do yet. Michael had planned everything, and had everything set, story boards and everything like that.

MARK: Did he do the choreography for "Billie Jean?"

JILL: I was told he did, because I had asked someone and I was told that he had done that one and the Motown special.

MARK: That was so incredible the way he went up on his toes, and those spins.

JILL: He's so talented, I can't imagine him taking dancing lessons from anyone.

MARK: How did you start working with Michael? What is your background?

JILL: My background is in photo styling. The photographer, Matthew Rolston, is very young. He's twenty-seven. He called me one day and he said "I'm going to shoot Michael Jackson and I've shot him once before, and I think that the two of you are going to really hit it off. He likes to be surrounded by young talent. Would you like to do this job?" And I said, "Oh, my God I'd love to .vork with Michael Jackson."

I went to the shooting for *Rolling Stone*, and that was the first time I had shot with him. And, people had told me, "Well he's very, very fussy about his clothes, so we may not have very much success with him. He may want to wear his own this or that." And he came in and ended up leaving having bought everything I brought to the shooting, which is unheard of. So that's how I got connected with him.

Then he started calling me. He has this personal bodyguard, Nelson, who would call and order this and that, and then we started doing shootings together.

MARK: When was the first time you met him, was it at the *Rolling Stone* shooting?

JILL: Yes, that was the first time I met him, at the *Rolling Stone* shooting. And I was amazed, I couldn't believe that was Michael when he walked in the door. He doesn't even look you in the eye when he first meets you, because he's so shy. I've never met somebody so shy before. It takes a long time before he'll look you in the eye when he's talking to you.

MARK: I met him at a party that was given for him in 1977 at Studio 54. He was very nice and polite, but in a way very withdrawn and timid.

JILL: Recently I've been collecting these pins for Michael, crests and crowns, and jeweled pins from a friend of mine who's a jewelry designer in town, and she collects old pins. I looked at them and brought back about fifty of them for Michael. And she ran into him at an old antique store in Hollywood, and she was so excited, because she's a big fan of his, and she knew that her pins had been going to him. She ran over and said, "My friend Jill has been collecting my pins for you." And he goes, "Oh, yeah, they're real nice. Thank you." And then he turned and walked away. She was so upset, and I tried to explain to her that's Michael, he's just very shy, and to be approached like that with a lot of enthusiasm from someone he doesn't know, his response is to be shy. Sometimes people take it as being aloof, he's really just shy . . . very shy.

MARK: It must be very exciting to be working with the hottest recording star in the world today.

JILL: It is. You know, when we first started working together, the new album wasn't out yet, and he had just finished the "E.T." album that he did with Steven Spielberg, and he brought the demo to "Thriller" and we listened to the album over and over again. Each shooting I've been on we've played that album. And, at that time "Beat It," which is the first song on the second side, was and still is my favorite song off of the album. And I used to say to him stuff like, "That's gonna be a big hit, Michael! That one's it!" And he'd say, "You think so?" like my word would mean anything in the record industry! And I said, "Yeah, that's it, that's the big hit!" It's funny, because I've seen what has happened to his album, because it started out as just a tape that he played in the studio.

MARK: Who else have you worked with?

JILL: I worked a lot with Rick Springfield, Lionel Richie, Kenny Rogers, a lot of

T.V. people: Linda Evans, Linda Carter, Linda Gray. I just got interviewed for *People* magazine, because I have a line of baby clothes. I don't know if Suzan told you that.

MARK: She told me that you do some designing.

JILL: Yes, I design baby clothes. But it's a fun job to help mold someone's image, and I feel like I've had a nice part in Michael's whole look, his new look.

MARK: Did you have anything to do with the Motown TV special?

JILL: No. All of the stage stuff is done by one of his sister-in-laws, she does a great job for them too. I think that they looked real good on stage on the Motown special. They each have their own personalities, and are extremely different. There is no one person colliding into the other one's "look." Except for Michael, they all know exactly what they'll wear and what they won't wear, and they tend to want the *flashiest* things that you can put together. I did a shooting of all six of *The Jacksons* right before the Motown special, which is where that one shot of Michael in the yellow vest is from, and there is one shot of them all in grey and yellow and white, and it's a beautiful shot, real casual and real pretty. And that's a real chore to get all of them together, and keep them all happy!

MARK: Do you have anything else lined up for him?

JILL: Not specifically.

MARK: Is there anything that you can tell me about Michael, that would be of interest to his fans?

JILL: People always ask me questions about Michael. He's probably one of the most natural and exciting artists that I've ever had the pleasure to work with, and as far as style, I don't know anyone who has as much style as Michael. He's like a mannequin. I don't know if you know this, but Michael has mannequins up at the house. He opens himself up like a mannequin, and he respects everyone that he brings in to work with him as an artist. And he just lets everyone do their thing; he goes along with it. Because, even though he is a superstar, he respects everyone for what they do. He'll ask questions in a shooting, he'll say, "How did you know that I would like this with that?" He talks to you as if what you're doing is just as special as what he's doing, and I really get that from Michael. He respects everyone as an artist themselves. I couldn't say enough good things about Michael Jackson. He's really a pleasure. He gets as much of a kick out of what I'm doing as I do from him. It's a nice twist. There's no attitude with Michael, no attitude at

139

all. The only thing that is interpreted as attitude with Michael is his shyness.

And that's how Michael has been getting all his visual panache lately—with his excellent taste and the assistance of Jill Klein!

11

The "Say, Say, Say" Saga

On October 3, 1983, the much awaited Paul McCartney/ Michael Jackson duet "Say, Say, Say" was released to radio stations across the country. Produced by George Martin, one version of it appeared on Paul's album "Pipes Of Peace," and another one was re-mixed for discos and dance clubs and lengthened to five minutes and forty seconds.

When it came time for the re-mixing of the song, Paul McCartney and George Martin decided to enlist the services of the most highly reputed and successful disco mix experts on either side of the Atlantic, John "Jellybean" Benitez. Known as the Number One record mixer in the business, twenty-five-year-old Benitez has recently worked on such Number One record smashes as Billy Joel's "Tell Her About It," Michael Sembello's "Maniac," Irene Cara's "What A Feeling

(Theme From "Flashdance")," and Madonna's "Holiday" which he also produced.

To keep in touch with what is happening on the dance club scene, Benitez "spins" records on Friday and Saturday nights at the popular New York City disco, The Funhouse. Perched above the dancefloor on weekends, John is able to see exactly what the crowds respond to, and when he is in the studio he works on obtaining the hottest sound possible to put down on vinyl.

According to "Jellybean," the time that he spent working on the McCartney/Jackson material was a dream come true. He commented that "Say, Say, Say" and "The Man" (the other Michael and Paul 1983 collaboration) were two of his favorite projects and reported that, "Both of these cuts are more dance-oriented than 'The Girl Is Mine,' and gave me more room to work. 'Say, Say, Say' was my favorite, and the interplay between Paul and Michael's vocals is great. Obviously, Michael's voice gives McCartney more room to play around and more space for his voice too. It was one of my favorite sessions thusfar, because they're both huge personal favorites of mine. I'd like to see them do a whole album together, because they work so well together. I feel that Michael definitely is making Paul move, and what they're producing together in these sessions is definately 'dance' music. Through it all, both of their distinctive styles come through beautifully, and I can't wait to work with them again!"

On Sunday October 2, the day before the special twelve-inch Benitez re-mix went into official distribution, I met with "Jellybean" and his publicist, David Salidor. John was on his way to Kennedy International Airport, headed for London where he was set to work on a new record by the group *"B" Movie* for Sire Records. At seven o'clock that evening a long silver Cadillac limousine pulled up in front of my Manhattan apartment, and it was there, riding in the luxury automobile that I conducted my interview about "Say, Say, Say," Paul McCartney and Michael Jackson, and their other Benitez-mixed duet "The Man." As the New York City skyline sank into the distance out the back window of the limo, our conversation proceeded like this:

MARK: Is Madonna still Number One this week?

JOHN: Yes, six weeks as Number One, on all three top radio stations in New York, above Lionel Richie, above Talking Heads; everybody. It's Number One on WBLS, WKTU, "KISS" (WRKS). It's still Number One in *Billboard* after four weeks! I have the Number One, the Number Two, the Number Eight, and the Number Ten records on the "Dance" charts in this week's *Billboard*. Irene Cara was a Number One record, and this (he said holding up the British 12" single version of "Say, Say, Say") will be another Number One record.

MARK: Now this is the British version of "Say, Say, Say?"

JOHN: Yes.

MARK: And when will this be released?

JOHN: It was released promotionally on Thursday (September 29, 1983) "World-wide." Paul McCartney has a "World-wide" release date. And Monday, (October 3, 1983) it will be released commercially to the stores.

MARK: Tell me about your work on "Say, Say, Say."

JOHN: I was contacted by MPL Communications in England, which is Paul McCartney's company. I received a call from Mickey Eichner from Columbia Records; well actually I got a call from my attorney that Mickey Eichner had called him, and that I would be getting a call from McCartney. Alan Crowder called me from MPL, and asked if I'd be interested in mixing two, possibly three songs on the forthcoming McCartney album; two of which would feature Michael Jackson. And, I was like in shock! (he laughed).

I mean, the amount of records these two guys have sold, Paul with *The Beatles* and by himself, and Michael with the *Jackson Five* and by himself. Michael's "Thriller" sold over fourteen million copies on its own! He's like the biggest-selling artist for an album ever, since *The Bee Gees* ("Saturday Night Fever").

MARK: Well, Carole King is the only one that's topped him, and that's at fifteen million for "Tapestry." But at this rate Michael is going to break her record. At the moment he is the biggest-selling male in the history of recorded music, topping Elvis, Frank Sinatra . . .

DAVID: Well, you ought to know!

JOHN: Anyway, they called me and told me that they were sending me the "masters," two 48-track mixes. That was on August 16th, about 5:00 a.m., I was still asleep!

On "Say, Say, Say" I started that on Thursday, August 25th, on the "master" tape. And the first day, at Sigma Sound I was just listening to the tape, to see . . . because it was 48 tracks, so usually on the first day, I go in and get all of the "EQ's" which are the sounds, and start doing all of the "mutes" where things come in and out. When you're doing 48 tracks, it's really a lot more involved than doing 24.

There was so much security surrounding this project. Usually, they'll give me a tape of a project. But the only way I could listen to this one was to go to Mickey Eichner's office, who's the Vice President of A&R (Artists & Repertoire) at Columbia. And, I could only listen to the tape with him in his office, I couldn't have a copy or anything. And the whole time I was in the studio, I had to be accompanied by Don

145

DeVito, the Vice President who handles all of the "A" artists on Columbia.

To do this was really strange, but there was just so much security. I guess they feared that someone would try to steal a tape and put it on the radio . . .

DAVID: Or bootleg it, or release it in advance of the official release, which has been known to happen.

JOHN: So I had a Vice President of Columbia just hanging out. He had to get up at eight o'clock in the morning, because I work days, I don't work at night.

So, I worked on the record on Friday (August 26th) again. I had total freedom on this. I was really surprised, first of all that they had sent the "masters" and they had made "safetys" (duplicate copies) and kept the "safetys" and sent me the actual "masters." Usually they keep the "masters" and send the "safetys." So, they let me do overdubs (additional effects) on the "masters," so I hired Ralph MacDonald to do the percussion overdubs. It was great, because Ralph was real helpful. He put congas down (on the tape), a cowbell, a tambourine, a shaker, because the song wasn't designed to be a dance number.

It's a danceable beat, but I guess since George Martin and Paul McCartney don't go to clubs, and just hear the dance records that are on the radio, maybe they don't understand what's really going on in the clubs. I put percussion on it, because I felt that maybe it would make the song move better. I worked on that the 25th and 26th, and on the following Monday, I went into the studio and finished "Say, Say, Say."

On the 29th, when I finished "Say, Say, Say," I started working on "The Man," which is the other Paul McCartney/Michael Jackson song which will be on the Paul McCartney album and there's a 12″ mix of that coming out, which is not on the album, but will probably be released when "Say, Say, Say" has peaked.

On "The Man," I didn't do any overdubs, and that features Michael Jackson as well. But, when you listen to the 7-inch version (45 rpm single), the whole first verse doesn't have any drums in it at all. In order to make it danceable, I had to take different drum sections from the other parts of the song and edit it all together, and there's like a million little pieces put together on the 12-inch.

I worked on that Monday and Tuesday, and on Wednesday I did a song called "Ode To A Koala Bear" which is only going to be released on the "B" side of the commercial 12-inch, I believe only in England, I'm not sure, I haven't seen a commercial copy (copies available to the public). It's not on the album, and that was a 24-track tape, and that was just McCartney without Jackson. It's a ballad, and it's about Koala Bears. I'm sure it will be a big hit in Australia and New Zealand!

MARK: So, on "Say, Say, Say" and "The Man," your dance re-mixes are only going to be available on the commercial 12-inch versions?

JOHN: Yes, and "Say, Say, Say" will be out tomorrow in the United States. "The Man" was supposed to be released in England, and "Say, Say, Say" was going to be released here. But I guess that they figured that with all of the imports coming back and forth, that they would have to release the same song.

DAVID: It was probably more of a marketing move to maximize sales . . .

JOHN: And to have it Number One all over the world at the same time.

MARK: How would you compare "Say, Say, Say" to the other things that Paul and Michael, solo and/or together have done?

JOHN: Well, this is more '80's sounding. I guess that when Paul did that song on Michael Jackson's album, "The Girl Is Mine," and saw how well it did in the clubs, he realized all of his stuff, even *The Beatles* songs, was danceable. This is more "R&B-ish." It's not "R&B," it's "pop," but with a steadier dance beat than probably anything else that he has done. I was really surprised that McCartney was doing a "dance" record. In the video version, Bob Giraldi had wanted to shoot to my mix of "Say, Say, Say," but they could only make a video that was three minutes long, and my mix is seven minutes long.

MARK: It was too long for the video that they had planned?

JOHN: Yes, they couldn't make a video for seven minutes, they wouldn't play it. They (TV programmers) would play it, but they would just play the first three or four minutes of it, and then turn it off.

MARK: So it's going to be a different mix on the video?

JOHN: I guess that it's going to be George Martin's mix.

MARK: So do you think that this signals some new direction for McCartney? Do you think that he's being influenced by Michael Jackson?

JOHN: Well, I don't know, I think that they made some type of mutual deal where they would each appear on the other's album. This way, McCartney is still capturing the youth market, as well as the older listeners.

DAVID: Why don't you tell Mark about your breakfast with McCartney?

JOHN: Well, I went to meet Alan Crowder at MPL Communications, in the Soho section of London, which is a drive. We got into a cab and went over to meet McCartney at the studio, and there was a film crew there, I guess that they were filming in another studio at the same time.

When I got there, there was no one there yet but Geoff Emerick

DAVID: *The Beatles'* engineer . . . and for *Supertramp* . . .

JOHN: I didn't know who he was, it didn't sink in. Then I met George Martin. This is at Air Studios. So, I was talking to George Martin, and he was telling me how much he really liked what I did, and the engineer, Emerick, was telling me that he was really into the work I had been doing, and that I really delivered a great mix. Usually you re-mix a dance record, and people don't really understand what you've done.

They were complimenting me on the mix, and I was just in awe. And then a guy walks in with glasses on and says, "Jelly! You must be Jelly!" I turned around, and then at that point, when I saw Paul, I suddenly realized he had been my favorite Beatle! It didn't really 'click' until that point.

Paul was very friendly, and complimentary about my mix. He told me that he was working with Bob Giraldi on the "Say, Say, Say" video, coming to New York first, and then he was going to L.A. to work on the video with Michael Jackson. And then he says to me about Michael, "I'm going to show that kid how to dance! I'm going to show him a few steps!" (he laughed).

We had coffee, and talked, and then he had to return to his recording session. But we talked for a good fifteen minutes. During that whole time I didn't realize that I was talking to Paul McCartney. It didn't register when I first met him and he was calling me "Jelly," in that Liverpool accent.

MARK: Have you had any personal contact with Michael since you contracted to re-mix "Say, Say, Say?"

JOHN: No, I haven't yet, but I can truthfully say that *The Jackson Five* has always been my favorite group.

MARK: I remember the first time I saw them, in October of 1969 when *The Supremes* hosted "The Hollywood Palace" and they introduced *The Jackson Five* for the first time. Do you remember the first time that you heard them, and the kind of impression you had?

JOHN: Yes, I was in the Seventh Grade, and I bought "I Want You Back!" It was like sixty-nine cents for the 45, and I was getting a seventy five cents a week allowance!

MARK: So, that was a major purchase at the time! That says a lot.

JOHN: And then "ABC" came out, and then their debut album came out. That was the only group that I can remember when I was growing up. I always was buying records, and I must have been twelve or thirteen-years-old when it came out.

MARK: And you had all those early *Jackson Five* records?

JOHN: Yes, I have every 7-inch single that *The Jacksons* have ever done, every album. I remember, I used to have this little portable record player, and I would bring records around out into the street when I was 12.

MARK: And you were playing D.J. back then with all of your *Jackson Five* 45's?

JOHN: Yes, I just remembered that!

MARK: What do you think of Michael on his own? What it your opinion of his musicianship as a singer, songwriter and performer?

JOHN: He's my favorite artist. He's had an influence on me, from my early record-buying experiences. He's really crossed a lot of barriers, as far as sound and being accepted with all kinds of audiences around the world. That song, "Beat It," AOR (Album Oriented Rock) radio stations were playing, and working with McCartney, and the song with Eddie Van Halen on it, and Vincent

Price. But, when I heard the "Off The Wall" album . . . and that was an incredible album! I was saying, "When 'Thriller' comes out, it will really have to be something to top it!" And it did!

DAVID: A lot of people didn't think that, even though "Thriller" was going to be good, it wouldn't be better than "Off The Wall," and it has been!

MARK: Michael incredibly surpassed himself with "Thriller," and it makes people wonder what's next!

JOHN: He had four "Top Ten" singles off of "Off The Wall," and five off of "Thriller." Are there any more singles left? I think that they have run out of "B" sides!

MARK: It was just released this week: "P.Y.T. (Pretty Young Thing)."

JOHN: You did a whole "Discography" on him, how many Number One records have *The Jacksons* had?

MARK: Eight Number One pop hits, and twenty singles in the "Top Ten."

DAVID: "ABC" is my favorite of their songs.

JOHN: "The Love You Save," that's my favorite song!

MARK: "I'll Be There" I've always been crazy about.

JOHN: There's a song that I play at The Funhouse called "Hum Along And Dance," which is from the "Get It Together" album.

MARK: That album is like a little-known "classic" of theirs.

JOHN: "Get It Together" is like a huge, huge Funhouse classic! Kids love it. If Motown ever re-released it, it would sell a lot in New York City! That was the first time that I ever heard a *Jacksons'* song played in a dance club. When was that released?

MARK: In 1973. "Dancing Machine" was originally on that album, and became such a big smash that they put it on a different album entitled "Dancing Machine" with new cuts on it.

JOHN: "Hum Along And Dance" I still think is just incredible, and I play it every Saturday. A lot of effects that are in it are being done in "dance" records now, and that was released years ago. And, none of *the Jacksons'* songs have any of those effects, you know, a lot of delay. It's eight minutes long, so there's a lot of breaks and stuff. It was one of the first "dance" mixes, without technically being one.

At that point the long grey Cadillac limousine pulled into Kennedy Airport and the conversation shifted from Michael Jackson to the flight arrangements.

David and I bid John "Bon voyage," and departed for the car. When we returned to Manhattan, David and I ran up to my apartment, and I proceeded to make myself a cassette copy of "Say, Say, Say." David left me to have my own personal preview session of the hit duet. For that evening I was one of the first people to have heard Michael's latest musical creation. The next morning, on the "Official International Release Date" Frankie Crocker's radio station, WBLS was already spinning "Say, Say, Say" for their listeners. Within days you couldn't turn on a radio without hearing the song . . . a 'sure sign that Michael Jackson, Paul McCartney *and* John "Jellybean" Benitez had another hot hit record on their hands!

12

Michael Talks About Michael

The majority of Michael's friends have show business careers. His closest friendship is still with Diana Ross.

"Diana is my best friend in the world. She's like a mother-lover-friend. She's the kind of person I can tell anything to. And she always tells me her most private secrets, too. That's the kind of relationship we have. We've stayed very close all these years."

Continues Michael of his list of favorite people, "Quincy Jones is a friend—even though when he invited me to a party at his house, I saw all these cars parked outside and freaked and left. But he understood. He's a true friend. Jane Fonda is a wonderful friend. She teaches me all kinds of stuff." Another great friend is Liza Minnelli. "She's like me, an old show biz kid. Add her to that list of my favorite people. I just love her to death. We get on the phone and we just gossip, gossip, gossip. What I like about Liza is that when we get together it's all show talk. I show her my favorite step and she shows me hers. She's a show-stopping performer too. She has real charisma. In the future I'd like to record her. I think a person like her should be heard on the radio and accepted and the whole thing. She's magic on stage."

"I love Steven Spielberg so much. I just love James Brown. He's phenomenal. I've never seen a performer create electricity with an audience like James Brown. He's got everybody in his hands and whatever he wants to do with them, he does it. It's amazing. I've always thought he was underrated. I love Sammy Davis Jr., I love Fred Astaire. I love George Lucas. I'm crazy about Katharine Hepburn." says Michael.

Another person whose accomplishments Michael idolizes is the late comedian, Charlie Chaplin. "I just love him to death!" exclaims Michael, "The little tramp, the whole gear and everything, and his heart—everything he portrayed on the screen was a truism. It was his whole life. He was born in London, and his father died an alcoholic when he was six. His mother was in an insane asylum. He roamed the streets of England, begging, poor, hungry. All this reflects on the screen and that's what I like to do, to bring all of those truths out. I love experienced people. I love people who are phenomenally talented. I love people who've worked so hard and been so courageous and are the leaders in their fields. For me to meet somebody like that and learn from them and share words with them—to me that's magic."

Since Michael's career so totally eclipses his brothers' successes how do they feel about his incredible superstardom? "The family enjoys what I do." Michael explains, "Each person in the group has a thing that he does. I sing and dance and the other brothers sing and dance, but I sing lead. A lot of interviewers and fans ask the brothers if they ever get jealous because Michael does this or he's out front all the time and they all scream for him a little more. It's a silly question, but it's interesting. When they ask me I just answer that they know what I do. I've been doing this since I was five years-old on stage and I feel it's something that God gave me to do. I'm the one who sings lead. They can sing lead but I've been chosen to sing lead on the songs and I'm thankful to be chosen. They kind of understand it, and they accept it because that's what I do."

"I would say the people who have influenced me the most were mainly Motown artists, but especially Stevie Wonder. I've learned so much from him. Sitting in on his sessions and talking to him and listening—he's just phenomenal! I had an interview with George Harrison in England, we did it together, and we got on the subject of Stevie. George said, his exact words were, 'Stevie Wonder—he makes me want to retire.' He said Paul McCartney feels the same way. You can't explain what Stevie does. The way he creates lyrics and melodies so effortlessly. He hears your voice, and even if you're trying to disguise it, he knows you. I'll come in the door and he'll start singing my name and just instantly create a song. It's incredible!"

Michael's idols also include, "Ray Charles, Jackie Wilson, Chuck Berry, and Little Richard—I think they had strong influences on a lot of people because these were the guys who really got rock 'n roll going. I like to start with the origin of things because it gets along, it changes. It's so interesting to see how it really was in the beginning."

"I love art!" Says Michael of another of his interests. "Whenever we go to Paris, I rush to the Louvre. I just never get enough of it. I go to all the museums around the world. I love art. I love it *too* much, because I end up buying everything and you become addicted. You see a piece you like and you say, 'Oh God, I've got to have this!' I love classical music. I've got so many different compositions. I guess when I was real small in kindergarten and hearing 'Peter and the Wolf' and stuff—I still listen to that stuff, it's great, and Boston Pops and Debussy, Mozart, I buy all that stuff. I'm a big classical fan. We've been influenced by all different kinds of music—classical, R & B, folk, funk—and I guess all those ingredients combined to create what we have now. I wouldn't be happy doing just one kind of music or labeling ourselves. I like doing something for everybody . . . I don't like our music to be labeled. Labels are like racism."

Michael's international fame can be a real hassle at times. "You don't get peace in a shop. If they don't know your name, they know your voice. And you can't hide."

"Being mobbed hurts," he continues. "You feel like you're spaghetti among thousands of hands. They're just ripping you and pulling your hair. And you feel that any moment you're gonna just break." Staying in hotels offers no escape. "Girls in the lobby, coming up the stairway. You hear guards getting them out of elevators. But you stay in your room and write a song. And when you get tired of that, you talk to yourself.

160

Then you let it all out onstage. *That's what it's like*!''

Michael laments that leaving his fortress-like home is also an obstacle, ''You'll drive outside and there'll be all these girls standing on the corner and they'll start bursting into screaming and jumping up and down and I'll just sink into my seat. That happens all the time. Everyone knew where we lived before, because it was on the 'Map To The Stars' Homes,' and they'd come around with cameras and sleeping bags and jump the fence, and sleep in the yard, and come in the house. We found people everywhere. It gets crazy. Even with twenty-four-hour guards, they find a way to slip in. One day my brother woke up and saw this girl standing over him in his bedroom. This one lady, who's thirty and crazy, and she said Jesus sent her there, and she got to me. People hitchhike and come to the house, and say they want to sleep with us, stay with us, and it usually ends up that one of the neighbors takes them in. We don't let them stay. We don't know them!''

Michael explains that he and his brothers are all highly self disciplined. ''I believe in God. We all do. We like to be straight, don't go crazy or anything. Not to the point of loosing our perspective on life, of what you are and who you are. A lot of entertainers, they make money and they spend the rest of their life celebrating that one goal they reached, and with that celebration comes the drugs and the liquor. And then they try to straighten up and they say, 'Who am I?' 'Where am I?' 'What happened?' and they've lost themselves, and they're broken. You have to be careful and have some kind of discipline. I'm not an angel, I know. I'm not like a Mormon or an Osmond or something where everything's straight. That can be silly sometimes.

"My career is mainly what I think about. There's been so many other things, they come in all the time. It's just hard to juggle your responsibilities around—my music here, my solo career, my movies there, T.V. and everything else." He'd like to get farther into producing, "There are people that I really like, that I want to do, like Diana. I don't just want to produce someone who has a good voice. It has to be someone who I like personally, because half of producing is coping with personality. A lot of people get in the studio and they throw this whole thing out at you. They're just hard to work with. I don't have much desire to deal with that."

Being on stage is still Michael's greatest release of tension, creativity, and anxiety. He elaborates, "I came on stage at Quincy's concert at the Rose Bowl. I did not want to go on stage. I was ducking and hiding and hoping he wouldn't see me hiding behind people when he called me on. Then I went up there and I just went crazy. I started climbing up a scaffold, the speakers, the light gear. The audience started getting into it and I started dancing and singing and that's what happens.

"I see dancing as the most wonderful thing of all time," he continues, "because people communicated through bodily movement before anything. Moving your body is an art. Dancing is really showing your emotions through bodily movement. It's a wonderful thing to get out on the floor and just feel free and do what you want to and just let it come out. When I dance, I *really* feel it and I just let my instincts take over. It's God. It's escapism, getting away from everything and just moving the body and letting all the tension and pain out. Just having a good time—that's what it's all about. I've always said this: discos will never die. People love to party, they love to dance, and you need rhythm, beat of the drum, to dance. That's how I feel. It will never die. Everybody dances, everybody clowns, and it's a wonderful thing!''

Is it any wonder why Michael creates such great dance music, if he truly feels this way?

On the subject of acting versus concert performing, how does Michael feel? ''I love both!'' he professes. ''Acting is the cream of the crop. I love performing, it's a phenomenal getaway. If you want to really let out everything you feel, that's the time to do it. With acting, it's like becoming another person. I think that's neat, especially when you totally forget. If you totally forget, which I love to do, that's when it's magic. I love to create magic—to put something together that's so unusual, so unexpected that it blows people's heads off. Something ahead of the times. Five steps ahead of what people are thinking. So people see it and say, 'Whoa . . . I wasn't expecting that!' I love surprising people with a present or a gift or a stage performance or anything. I love John Travolta, who came off that 'Kotter' show. Nobody knew he could dance or do all those things. He is like: BOOM! Before he knew it, he was the next big Brando or something.''

How about Broadway? That's the only arena that Michael hasn't stepped into. ''Not yet.'' he answers. ''I think it's good for sharpening your skills. It's the best for really reaching the zenith of your talent. You go so far and reach the peak of it and you say, 'Maybe this is the best performance I can do!' What's so sad about the whole thing is that you don't capture that moment. Look at how many great actors or entertainers have been lost to the world, because they did a performance one night, and that was it. With film, you capture that, it's shown all over the world, and it's there forever. Spencer Tracy will always be young in 'Captain's Courageous,' and I can learn and be stimulated by his performance. So much is lost in theater, so much. Or vaudeville. Do you know what I could have learned by watching all those entertainers? It would be unreal. That's what I hate about Broadway. I feel I'm giving a whole lot for nothing. I like to capture things and hold them there and share them with the whole world.''

Old movies are one of Michael's passions, he loves screenings of his favorites. ''There was a lot of great art, great acting, great directing, great stories. When it comes to stuff like 'Captain's Courageous,' or 'Boy's Town,' 'Father Flanagan,' 'Woman Of The Year'—that stuff is unreal. That's what's great about show business. It's escapism. You pay your five bucks to get in and sit there and you're in another world. Forget about the problems in the world. It's wonderful! It's entertaining! It's magic!''

Regarding his weekly vegetable juice fasts, Michael explains, ''It flushes out the system, cleans out the colon. I think that's great. To really make it work you have to do it properly. That's the sewer valve of the system. You have to keep that clean like you clean the outside of your body. All these impurities come out of your system because you're not clean inside. It comes out in pimples, or disease, or through big pores. Toxins trying to get out of your system. People should keep themselves clean.''

What is Michael's writing process like? ''I wake up from dreams and go, 'Wow! Put this down on paper!

The whole thing is strange. You hear the words, everything is right there in front of your face. And you say to yourself, 'I'm sorry, I just didn't write this. It's there already,' That's why I hate to take credit for the songs I've written. I feel that somewhere, someplace, it's been done, and I'm just a courier bringing it into the world. I really believe that. I love what I do. I'm happy at what I do. It's escapism.''

Well, all I can say is, if Michael Jackson is communicating with the spiritual world for the inspirational vibes for his songwriting, then he must sure have one hot Ouija Board to get these signals!

As an overview of everything that has happened to him in his life to date, how does Michael perceive it all? "I'd like to say that people in the world should really do what their hearts are set on. If they really believe a thing they should feel it through all the way, and then do it. The fact that *The Jacksons* have sold more than sixty million albums—I don't even know how many solo albums have sold—is proof that people can accomplish incredible things . . . no matter what your background. I'm going to be doing a lot of things for people in the future, from the heart. I want to thank everyone through the years, for the sixty million and everything. And I mean that. Thank you!''

Epilogue

"He's So Shy" was a huge hit record for *The Pointer Sisters*, but it could easily be interpreted as a song being sung about Michael Jackson.

Many of his closest friends and acquaintances have expressed their feelings that Michael is too sheltered for his own good. Diana Ross has tried to encourage him to be more outgoing, Jane Fonda has been instrumental in helping him break out of his shell, and people like Paul McCartney have done their best to get him over his feeling that the world is pushing in on him.

He admits, "I have a lot of trouble with friendships because I've spent so much of my life on stage. I don't always trust myself with regular people, so to speak. My idea of your average person is someone in a crowd who's running towards me trying to get my autograph or tear my clothes off. I still get afraid. It's a whole other life, and I haven't really experienced that. I was raised on stage and that's still where I'm the most comfortable. Everything else is foreign to me. I'm just beginning to know and learn about friendships.''

On Halloween night in 1979, Jane Fonda hosted a ''Disco Night'' at The Hollywood Palace, as a benefit for solar energy. Her guests were some of that year's biggest hit-makers: Michael Jackson, and *The Village People*. Randy Jones, the original cowboy from The Village People recalls that evening, ''We were working on the film 'Can't Stop The Music' at that time, and we were invited to perform by Jane Fonda. That was the first time I had ever met Michael Jackson. What I remember most is the fact that Michael spent a lot of time backstage off in a corner by himself. It's his shyness that I remember most.''

When I was researching this book, I spoke to many of Michael's friends in show business. One person who had a clear perspective on Michael was someone whom he had first met at the age of nine, Manhattan radio personality Frankie Crocker of WBLS-FM. When I spoke with Frankie recently in the studio of WBLS in mid-town Manhattan, we talked about Michael between ''On The Air'' segments.

Crocker had many fascinating and well-thought insights on Jackson, and tried to pinpoint the reason for his current universal popularity, from a radio programmer's viewpoint. Said Frankie, ''Michael has teamed up with what I believe is one of the most talented producers, Quincy Jones. And when you have a marriage of two very good talents, a producer who knows how to take a recording artist's wish, and being able to package it the way they did is a real success, and Michael being able to perform, and give the kind of performance that he does, has even made it more exciting.

"There is a mystique about Michael, that is also a feeling. They (the public) don't know exactly anything about Michael. Michael has been sheltered most of his life."

Analyzing the appeal of Michael's androgynous unisexual aura, Crocker admitted that the sense of mystery has only added interest. "That's always been that way, when Elton John said that he was 'bi,' it's been that way with Mick Jagger; they felt that way. There's some sort of appeal there, some sort of mystique. I'm not saying that Michael is, but I've heard it. There is a mystique. Who is his girlfriend? What is he? He's coming of age . . . what does he do? His hair, the way he dresses, the way he speaks . . . all of that. But it's all been positive."

"I think he was always shy," Frankie continues. "He was more outgoing when he was a youngster. But I think all of this attention and adolation that he was getting sort of did that to him. Because the public can do that, they can eat at an artist, and at a young age like that you can have an effect. The other kids were older, Michael was the youngest one, and since he was the lead, everybody asked him all these questions. I think somebody said something to him once possibly that could have made him respond, and be shy the way he is now.

"I think Michael is still growing up, I don't think he has had a chance. I don't think any artist really grows up in a way a kid in the street does. Any artist who makes that kind of money, and gets that kind of adulation that he gets, I don't think has a chance for him to grow up. First of all, the kid was a millionaire before he was fifteen-years-old, if he didn't have it in his hand, his father made sure he lived like it. He worked for it. Whatever they wanted they won . . . his brothers: Rolls Royces and Ferreri's when they were teenagers. And, I remember his father saying they bought a lot of land in California so his kids would never have to want anything. He was making sure that they were going to be secure. I don't think he ever went to a regular school outside of when he was in Gary, Indiana. He's had a tutor ever since I knew him, so that's isolation enough.''

Crocker projects into the future for Michael . . . Movies? ''I've seen him play in 'The Wiz' when he played that, but I don't know if he has any acting ability. He may surprise all of us, and one day just turn out to be a good leading man, another John Travolta-type. You never know with a superstar like that. It would be a departure and I think he would be well-received.''

What is it that lies ahead for Michael Jackson? His incredible video presentations of ''Billie Jean'' and ''Beat It'' all but set the airwaves on fire when they debuted on M-TV in the spring of 1983. Now with the filming of ''Thriller,'' and ''Say, Say, Say'' with Paul McCartney, it looks like a whole video album is possible, especially the way director Bob Giraldi has handled these videos of Michael's so far, with excitement and imagery.

In September of 1983, syndicated columnist Liz Smith ran the following item,

> *''Did you love* The Jackson Five? *Well, super-star MICHAEL JACKSON is re-uniting himself with his wonderful singing family and will take*

them on tour. They will be part of the concerts which begin across country after the New Year. In New York, both Radio City Music Hall and Madison Square Garden are already squared off, fighting to nab Michael and his show.''

So began the most excitedly anticipated concert tour of the decade, one in which Michael and *The Jacksons* would tour again with Jermaine for the first time since *The Jackson Five* ceased to exist in 1976.

Hopefully the ''Peter Pan'' project will materialize, but if not, it seems clear that motion pictures are the future for Michael, in addition to recording of course!

''My plan is to get into films,'' admits Michael. ''That's why I got so involved in the videos of 'Billie Jean' and 'Beat It.' Film is my dream. I love music and film and want to integrate them like it's never been done before.''

It's very rare that people all around the world agree on much, but in 1983 it was clear that people on the four corners of the Earth unanimously concur that they are all into Michael Jackson. Whether it's his hit records, his revolutionary videos, or his budding film career, one thing *is* for certain about that ''off the wall'' ''thriller'' . . . Michael Jackson is on top of the world, and that is just where he is going to stay!

Discography

ALBUMS:

Michael Jackson with The Jackson Five:

— "Diana Ross Presents The Jackson Five"
   (Motown) 1969*
— "ABC" (Motown) 1970*
— "Third Album" (Motown) 1970
— "The Jackson Five Christmas Album"
   (Motown)*
— "Maybe Tomorrow" (Motown) 1971
— TV Soundtrack: "Goin' Back To Indiana"
   (Motown) 1971*

*"Gold" album (for 500,000 units sold in the U.S.)

—"The Jackson Five's Greatest Hits" (Motown) 1971*
—"Lookin' Through The Windows" (Motown) 1972*
—"Skywriter" (Motown) 1973
—"Get It Together" (Motown) 1973
—"Dancing Machine" (Motown) 1974*
—"Moving Violation" (Motown) 1975
—"Joyful Jukebox Music" (Motown) 1975
—"The Jackson Five Anthology" (3-record set) (Motown) 1976*
—"Boogie" (Natural Resources/Motown) 1979
—"Motown Superstar Series Volume 12: The Jackson Five" (Motown) 1980
—"Michael Jackson & The Jackson Five: Great Songs And Performances That Inspired The Motown 25th Anniversary T.V. Special" (Motown) 1983

Michael Jackson with The Jacksons:

—"The Jacksons" (Epic/Philadelphia International) 1976*
—"Goin' Places"(Epic/Philadelphia International) 1977
—"Destiny" (Epic) 1978**
—"Triumph" (Epic) 1978
—"The Jackson's Live" (2-record set) (Epic) 1981

*"Gold" album (for 500,000 units sold in the U.S.)
**"Platinum" album (for 1,000,000 units sold in the U.S.)

Michael Jackson with The Jackson Five *on compilations and other albums, performing material not found anywhere else:*

- —"Motown At The Hollywood Palace" (Motown) 1970
  Live performances of "I Want You Back" and medley: "Sing A Simple Song/Can You Remember"
- —"Diana: TV Soundtrack" (Motown) 1971
  The Jackson Five sing two "live" medleys: "Mama's Pearl/Walk On By/The Love You Save" and "I'll Be There/Feelin' Alright." Michael and his brothers also are featured in a skit with Diana Ross and Bill Cosby.
- —"The Motown Story" (Motown) 1970
  Michael talks about his life in *The Jackson Five*
- —"Motown Superstars Sing Motown Superstars" (Motown) 1983
  previously unreleased "Ask The Lonely" by *The Jackson Five*

MICHAEL JACKSON:

- —"Got To Be There" (Motown) 1972
- —"Ben" (Motown) 1972*
- —"Music & Me" (Motown) 1973

*"Gold" album (for 500,000 units sold in the U.S.)

—''Forever,Michael'' (Motown) 1975
—''The Best Of Michael Jackson'' (Motown) 1975
—''Off The Wall'' (Epic) 1979*
—''Motown Superstar Series Volume 7: Michael Jackson'' (Motown) 1980
—''One Day In Your Life'' (Motown) 1981
—''E.T. The Extra-Terrestrial Storybook'' (MCA) 1982
—''Thriller'' (Epic) 1982*
—''Thriller'' (The Picture Disc) (Epic) 1983
—''Thriller'' (Half-speed Master Version) (Epic) 1983

Michael on Movie Soundtracks:

—''The Wiz'' (2-record set) (MCA) 1978

SINGLES:

Michael Jackson with The Jackson Five*:*

—''I Want You Back'' (Motown) 1969**
—''ABC'' (Motown) 1970**†
—''The Love You Save'' / ''Found That Girl'' (Motown) 1970**

*''Platinum'' album (for 1,000,000 units sold in the U.S.)
**''Platinum'' single (for 2,000,000 units sold in the U.S.)
†Grammy Award-winner

—"I'll Be There" (Motown) 1970**

—"Mama's Pearl" (Motown) 1971*

—"Never Can Say Goodbye" (Motown) 1971*

—"Maybe Tomorrow" (Motown) 1971

—"Sugar Daddy" (Motown) 1971*

—"Little Bitty Pretty One" (Motown) 1972

—"Lookin' Through The Windows" (Motown) 1972

—"Corner Of The Sky" (Motown) 1972*

—"Hallelujah Day" (Motown) 1973

—"Get It Together" (Motown) 1973

—"Dancing Machine" (Motown) 1974**

—"Whatever You Got, I Want" (Motown) 1974

—"I Am Love (Part I & II)" (Motown) 1975

—"Forever Came Today" (Motown) 1975

Michael Jackson with THE JACKSONS:

—"Enjoy Yourself" (Epic) 1976*

—"Show You The Way To Go" (Epic/Philadelphia International) 1977

—"Goin' Places" (Epic/Philadelphia International) 1977

—"Blame It On The Boogie" (Epic) 1978

—"Shake Your Body Down To The Ground)" (Epic) 1979**

—"Lovely One" (Epic) 1980

*"Gold" single (for 1,000,000 units sold in the U.S.)
**"Platinum" single (for 2,000,000 units sold in the U.S.)

—"Heartbreak Hotel" (Epic) 1980
—"Can You Feel It" (Epic) 1981
—"Walk Right Now" (Epic) 1981

MICHAEL JACKSON & DIANA ROSS:

—"Ease On Down The Road" (MCA) 1978

MICHAEL JACKSON & PAUL McCARTNEY:

—"The Girl Is Mine" (Epic) 1982*
—"Say, Say, Say" (Epic) 1983

MICHAEL JACKSON:

—"Got To Be There" (Motown) 1971*
—"Rockin' Robin" (Motown) 1971*
—"I Wanna Be Where You Are" (Motown) 1972
—"Ben" (Motown) 1972**
—"With A Child's Heart" (Motown) 1973
—"We're Almost There" (Motown) 1975
—"Just A Little Bit Of You" (Motown) 1975
—"You Can't Win (Part 1)" (Epic) 1979
—"Don't Stop 'Til You Get Enough" (Epic) 1979**†

*"Gold" single (for 1,000,000 units sold in the U.S.)
**"Platinum" single (for 2,000,000 units sold in the U.S.)
†Grammy Award-winner

—"Rock With You" (Epic) 1979*
—"Off The Wall" (Epic) 1979*
—"She's Out Of My Life" (Epic) 1980*
—"One Day In Your Life" (Motown) 1980
—"Billie Jean" (Epic) 1983*
—"Beat It" (Epic) 1983*
—"Wanna Be Stratin' Something" (Epic) 1983*
—"Human Nature" (Epic) 1983
—"P.Y.T. (Pretty Young Thing)" (Epic) 1983

MICHAEL JACKSON 12" Disco Re-mixes:

—"Billie Jean" (Epic) 1983
—"Wanna Be Startin' Something' " (Epic) 1983
—"Say, Say, Say" (with Paul McCartney) (Epic) 1983

MICHAEL JACKSON "Guest" Appearances:

As Producer:

—"Night Time Lover" on the LaToya Jackson debut album "LaToya Jackson" (Polydor) 1980
—"Muscles" on the Diana Ross album "Silk Electric" (RCA) 1982

*"Gold" single (for 1,000,000 units sold in the U.S.)

As A Guest Duet Artist:

—''On the Paul McCartney album ''Pipes of
Peace'' (Columbia) 1983
''Say, Say, Say,'' with Paul McCartney
''The Man'' with Paul McCartney

ABOUT THE AUTHOR

Mark Bego is currently Editor-In-Chief of the oldest and most famous show business fan magazine in existence, "Modern Screen." A native of Detroit, Michigan; his interest in show business has led him to become one of New York City's top entertainment writers.

Mark is the author of three published books: "Barry Manilow" (Grosset & Dunlap/Tempo Books 1977), "The Captain & Tennille" (Grosset & Dunlap/Tempo Books 1977), and "The Doobie Brothers" (Popular Library 1980).

Bego has critiqued records and concerts, reviewed Broadway shows, covered the Manhattan nightlife circuit, and interviewed media stars (including Rod Stewart, Cher, Katharine Hepburn, and Donna Summer) for such publications as "People," "US," "After Dark," "Billboard," "Record World," and "Cue/New York" to name a few.

Mark appeared weekly for two years as an on-camera reviewer and interviewer on the Manhattan television show "Tomorrow's Television Tonight," and as a host and producer of his own TV special "Profile." He was the producer/performer/host of recent New York City stage shows "Casino Evil" and "Stupid Cupid." His articles in "Modern Screen" are read around the world.